MW01273169

Travel to Anguilla, Caribbean Beauty

Vacation Destination

Author
Thomas Bailey.

Publisher:
SONIT
2162 Davenport House, 261 Bolton Road. Bury. Lancashire. BL8 2NZ. United Kingdom.

Table of Content

Summary

Traveling and Tourism

Tourism is a global industry, which involves people travelling across the world for a variety of reasons mainly recreation and sightseeing. When tourists decide where to travel, they often base their decisions on the attractions and situations in a city or country. Sometimes countries are in the midst of political unrest, such as war, civil war or terrorism. Tourists will avoid these destinations, choosing more peaceful destinations instead. However, while they are there, unforeseen situations may occur, such as tsunamis, natural disasters, diseases or accidents. It is important for tourism professionals and for tourists themselves to adequately prepare, through thorough research, before they (or their clients) leave on a journey.

Every country has sights of attractions and places of interest, some of which are not known that easy, and to discover them, you have to need a guide on the interested place, learn about local people's attitude and relation with foreginers, it is important to know all these. This is the importance of Tourist Book Guide

Introduction

The flat island of Anguilla stretches 16 miles across and 3 miles wide at its fattest point. At the tallest peak, Crocus Hill, the island reaches up to about 215 feet above sea level. Anguilla is the most northern of the Leeward Islands in the Lesser Antilles, situated directly north of St. Martin. The limestone structure of the island provides for many caves and other natural formations that attract tourists from around the world, as well as historical points of interest and buzzing nightlife entertainment.

Attractions

West central Anguilla offers a variety of attractions to appease any traveler. Located in The Valley, in the central portion of the map, the Wallblake House is a historical plantation home with a connected museum that claims to be the oldest building in Anguilla. Patrons can get a great taste of the past by visiting this structure, built by Will Blake in 1787.

Another historic landmark is the Old Salt Factory and Pumphouse, which sits on the southwestern side of The Valley. Salt played a major role in Anguilla's history, and a tour of the factory gives great insight to the industry that was once flourishing on the island. Interestingly, the Pumphouse has been renovated into one of Anguilla's most popular nightlife attractions. Also located near The Valley, visitors will find the tallest point on the island at Crocus Hill. Here you can tour the remains of the Crocus Hill Prison, which offers great views of the island.

On the northeastern side of the island, tourists can check out the Heritage Museum Collection at Pond Ground. The museum houses interesting artifacts that range from ancient Arawak Indian tools to household items used by 19th century settlers. Head a bit further north, and you'll come across a section of rainforest that offers a great hiking trail.

Near Shoal Bay, explorers will revel in the natural wonder of the Fountain Cavern National Park. Make your way 50 feet down a cave to two fresh water pools and plentiful petroglyphs and rock carvings. This site is believed to have been a center of religious worship by the Amerindians, and combines the great outdoors with a taste of Anguilla's history.

For a truly unique experience, you should check out Anguilla's impressive hydroponic farm. Created by CuisinArt's Dr. Howard Resh to provide the infertile island with an alternative to importing produce, the farm has become the only one of its kind in the world. Housed on the property of the CuisinArt Resort and Spa near the West End of Anguilla, this facility grows everything from peppers, tomatoes and onions to bok choy, water dress and mint oregano. Guests can enjoy a tour of this fantastic greenhouse, then head over to the resort's restaurant to taste some of the great produce in action.

Places to Stay

The Valley

Centrally located on the map, The Valley is one of the most popular places to stay on Anguilla. It is the hub of all government activity, and offers a variety of restaurants, art and nightlife. Be sure to check out the Anguilla Arts and Crafts Center for a taste of the island's creative culture. The Village is also home to the Anguilla Natural Trust Museum, as well as previously mentioned attractions like the Wallblake House.

Shoal Bay

The area of Shoal Bay offers something for everyone. On the western half of the bay, guests can enjoy themselves at the many beach-side bars and tasty barbecue shacks that fill the streets. Those seeking a more secluded experience should head to the eastern portion of Shoal Bay, which is much less crowded and offers an ideal spot for leisurely snorkeling and sunbathing. Offshore islands like Sandy Isle and Prickly Pear provide excellent getaways for those looking to escape for the day.

Sandy Ground Village

This two-mile stretch of Anguilla is one of the most exciting places to stay in Anguilla. Not only is it home to the Old Salt Factory and Pumphouse, this area offers the most popular beachfront access on the island. Guests will find many restaurants and bars lined along the picture-perfect shoreline of Sandy Ground. There are also many places that provide rental equipment for water-sports like snorkeling, parasailing and more. The accommodations here are very low-key, and offer a retreat away from bustling resorts. From Sandy Ground, tourists can hop on a quick boat ride to the Prickly Pear Cays that boast rows of beach chairs and an on-site restaurant.

Rendezvous Bay and West End

This area (in the lower left portion of the map) is also popular with tourists. You'll find a number of great lodging options, as well as plentiful dining options, attractions and nightlife entertainment. Many art galleries are located in the vicinity, as well as charming shops. One of the most popular spots in Rendezvous Bay is the Dune Preserve, where patrons can enjoy a tropical-themed beach bar with live music and excellent views of the seaside.

Transportation

Clayton J. Lloyd International Airport (AXA) is not a major international airports, notwithstanding its impressive sounding name. The airport has frequent commercial flights to and from several Caribbean destinations, including Puerto Rico, Antigua and St. Martin. If you are arriving from the United States or a more distant location, you'll probably make a connection through one of the region's larger airports.

Ferries are a popular mode of transportation for vacationers looking to visit Anguilla's neighboring island of St. Martin. At the Blowing Point Ferry Terminal, guests can catch a ride to St. Martin or the Dutch side of St. Maarten. The ferry shuttles run throughout the day.

Anguilla Past and Present

Anguilla in the Past and in the Present

Anguilla's past has impacted in the island's present economy and culture

The history of Anguilla strays away from the beaten path of other islands in the Caribbean, though it does share some similarities with its neighbors. The roots of Anguilla's heritage begin with the Amerindians who came to the island long before Europeans claimed the land in the name of their home countries.

History

English settlers came to Anguilla around 1650 and began establishing colonies on the island. At about 35 square miles, Anguilla is approximately half the size of Washington D.C. with flat, low-lying land. All though British explorers attempted to cultivate cash crops and large plantations to gain money and power from the land, Anguilla did not turn out to be as profitable a settlement as the explorers had hoped. Due to the island's thin soil, arid climate, and unpredictable rainfall, growing large amounts of major cash crops was very difficult.

This made establishing the massive plantations that were so popular in the rest of the Caribbean virtually impossible. African slaves were brought to the island, but since there were no plantations to be farmed, many of the English settlers left in search of more profitable ventures elsewhere in the region. Even today, agriculture is not a profitable one, with major natural resources being lobster, fish, and salt.

After Europeans abandoned Anguilla in search of more profitable land, the black slaves were left on the island, and some bought land from their former masters. Thus, some blacks enjoyed the freedom of making a living for themselves even before the British officially emancipated them. The mixture of African and European heritage on Anguilla has created a unique and rich culture.

Culture

The culture on Anguilla is filled with interesting facets, including the islanders' past and present religious practices, their holidays and celebrations, and their efforts to preserve their heritage and history. Years of trying to communicate with plantation owners caused many Africans to lose their native tongue, and to this day English remains the official language of Anguilla. One way slaves had of preserving their heritage was to incorporate their traditional cuisine with those foodsources available on the island. This helped to create the unique style of Caribbean food, which includes mixtures of African, Creole, and European dishes, as well as some that are wholly unique to the islands. With over 70 restaurants in Anguilla, visitors can easily find and sample many of these dishes.

Today, Anguilla is an island of peace and tranquility, but it has not always been so. The political structure of Anguilla has weathered various conflicts. Today Anguilla's government is based around a parliamentary representative democratic dependency. This means that the head of government is the Chief Minister (similar to a Prime Minister), and decisions are made by a multi-party parliament.

Economy

The island's economy began with independent islanders taking up seafaring jobs to provide for themselves, and moved to an economy that relies on revenue from the tourism industry. The past decade has seen the number of tourists visiting the island increase significantly each year. However, visitors stopping in for day trips from other islands or on excursions off cruise ships has not increased much. This is because many large cruise ships pass up Anguilla for other islands that are better known for larger ports and duty-free shopping. Those who do visit the island tend to stay for the tranquility afforded by Anguilla's 33 beaches, rather than shopping opportunities or attractions. These visitors also typically stay for anywhere between three to eight days.

Whether you choose to visit Anguilla for a day or stay for a week, you are sure to discover that past events have shaped the island's present, creating the perfect culture for vacationers to enjoy.

Culture

The Culture of Anguilla

Many historical events have impacted the current culture of Anguilla

Anguilla's culture has been shaped by its rich and unique heritage, which includes the settlements of the island's first people, the Amerindians, the European settlers who originally came to the Caribbean in search of riches, and the African slaves who were imported to Anguilla to work on the colonists' plantations.

Religious Practices

A group of Amerindians known as the Arawak Indians were the first people to practice religion on Anguilla. This group of indigenous people based their religious beliefs on the sun, moon, and two large caverns located on the island, where the Indians believed humans came from. The Arawaks held various religious ceremonies in the Big Springs and The Fountain caverns. Today, artifacts and other evidence of the Arawaks' religious practices can still be seen in the two caverns, including petroglyphs and offering bowls.

In the present day, the population of Anguilla practices several different organized religions, and the islanders are largely of the Christian faith. There is a church almost every two miles on the island. The majority of the people on the island are Anglican, which makes up 40 percent of the people's religion. The next most popular denomination on Anguilla is Methodist, which accounts for approximately 33 percent of religion on the island. Other religions that have found a home on the island are Seventh Day Adventists, Baptists, Roman Catholic, and miscellaneous religious practices.

Celebrations and Holidays

Anguilla has a number of annual festivals and holidays, most of which celebrate important historical events that have helped to shape the island's culture. The most spectacular cultural celebration on the island is the annual Summer Festival. This event is held in August and begins on a Monday at 5:00 a.m. with an early-morning jam called the J'Ouvert Mornin. This festival celebrates the emancipation of African slaves on Anguilla. The festivities includes dancing, parades, fairs, and other colorful events. During this and other festivals, the days consist of picnics on the beach as well as sailboat racing, which is Anguilla's national sport.

Sailboat racing is as important and celebrated on Anguilla as cricket is on other Caribbean islands. The islanders hold the first sailboat race of the season on Easter Monday. Sailboat racing on the island is a special event, and hundreds of local people, as well as tourists, gather round the island shores to witness the breathtaking race take place.

Anguilla also celebrates some English holidays, like the Queen's Birthday and Whit Monday. These events are evidence of British culture's mark on the island. Another special day for Anguillans is May 30, which is when the islanders celebrate Anguilla Day. On May 30, 1967 the St. Kitts police were forced off of Anguilla, and there was peace on the island.

Preserving Culture

In 1989, under the ANT ACT, the Anguilla National Trust was established in order to preserve the island's heritage, natural resources, and culture so that future generations can experience the rich heritage and cultural resources of Anguilla. With their home office opening in 1991, ANT has been protecting Anguilla heritage for many years. They have a number of different programs that serve as custodians over Anguilla's natural environment and archaeological sites, which are an important part of the country's history and played a major part in shaping the island's culture.

ANT diligently oversees the operation of Anguilla's national parks, protected areas, and museums, and also educates the public about the importance of the island's natural resources and historical sites.

Economy

The Economy of Anguilla

Anguilla's economy has moved towards the tourism industry in recent years

Anguilla's unique climate made it impossible for early English colonists to cultivate the plantation lifestyle on the island. Therefore, Anguilla never fell in with one of the most popular economic trends in the Caribbean region of that time period: the growth and export of sugarcane. Currently, the island has followed many Caribbean islands by becoming increasingly dependent on tourism as a major source of income.

First Economic Practices

Anguilla economics began with the arrival of the the Arawak Indians, who came from South America to settle on the island. Most of the Arawak's economic endeavors consisted of self-sustaining farming to feed and clothe their families, as opposed to bartering and trade for profit. The Indians produced crops of cotton, corn, and sweet potatoes. British settlers made attempts at turning Anguilla into a plantation island, but the island's unpredictable rainfall, arid climate, and soil, which was a thin layer over a limestone base, was not conducive for big sugarcane plantations.

Going into the 1800's, Anguilla's economy was based on the cultivation of rum, sugar, cotton, indigo, fustic, and mahogany plantations. African slaves were brought to Anguilla to work on these farms, but the island could not sustain large-scale sugar plantations and other crops.

Soon the colonists found out that plantation farming was not very profitable on Anguilla, and most settlers abandoned the unprofitable plantations to make money on other islands in the Caribbean. The African slaves were left on the island, and some masters sold their land to slaves, who took up a peasant-like lifestyle on Anguilla. Those who remained on the island took up fishing and and other seafaring trades to make a living.

Today's Economy

Today, Anguilla's economy has taken the same route as many other tropical islands: tourism. People from all over the world come to visit the region's beautiful beaches and other tourist attractions. Although Anguilla has several natural resources from which the island's economy makes some money, it relies heavily on income from luxury tourism.

Anguilla's other sources of income include offshore banking, lobster fishing, and contributions from emigrants to the island. In recent years, Anguillan officials have put a lot of effort into developing Anguilla's offshore financial sector, which has grown consistently. By diversifying its economy, Anguilla won't have to rely so heavily on one main source of income. A 2001 poll found that there were 6,049 people in the Anguillan labor force. Most of the island's workers are employed in the field of commerce (36 percent), with the service industry making up about 29 percent of the labor force. Other areas of the job force are the construction industry, which employs about 18 percent of the working islanders, transportation and utilities (about 10 percent), and agriculture, forestry, and mining (about 4 percent). Manufacturing makes up the rest of the island's job market.

The substantial growth of the tourism industry on Anguilla has caused a spark in the field of construction. New hotels and other tourist destinations are being built on the island, which means more work in the construction business. The overall impact of the ever-expanding tourism industry has been a positive one for Anguilla's economy.

Events & Festivals

Anguilla's Events and Festivals

From sporting events to cultural celebrations, Anguilla offers up a variety of events and festivals

There's just something about a street festival that brings people together, and showcases the best of what a place has to offer. In Anguilla, visitors have the opportunity to attend numerous cultural celebrations throughout the year. These events range from regatta galas to art festivals.

Cultural Celebrations

In March, there is an Easter celebration in Anguilla where all roads lead to Island Harbour. Festival Del Mar provides the Anguillian people with the opportunity to celebrate the island's rich history while offering visitors a window into the cultural traditions. This festival celebrates all things of the sea; there are traditional cooking and culinary competitions where only seafood recpes are accepted. There are also fishing tournamets, swimming races and boatracing.

Much like many other islands in the Caribbean, Anguilla celebrates the emancipation of slaves with an event. In Anguilla, however, the celebration lasts for 11 days. This event is called the Anguilla Summer Festival and takes place in the middle of each summer. Activities include live music, three beauty pageants, a boat race, a parade, and more.

In the Caribbean, there is no event more widespread than the celebration of Carnival. This celebration typically occurs in the days before lent, however in Anguilla, the festivities take place in August, and are known as Jouvert Morning (or August Day). On Jouvert Morning, islanders rise early, and dance through the streets. This event is a part of the Anguilla Summer Festivals, which begins in July and runs through August. Activities include beauty pageants, boat races, street festivals, and beach parties.

Sporting Events

The Anguilla Open Golf Tournament takes place at CuisinArt Golf Resort & Spa, and invites more than 100 golfers from around the Caribbean and the United States to compete for a championship title worth several thousand dollars. The event takes place in June and includes three rounds of golf, lunches during play, and opening and closing ceremonies.

In May, boats fill Road Bay for several races as a part of the Anguilla Regatta. On land, beach parties take place at Sandy Ground over a three day period.

The sporty, charity-minded set won't want to miss participating in the Anguilla Optimist Race Against AIDS in November. Participants can walk, jog, or run in a 5K, 10K, or half marathon the day before International World AIDS Day.

Music Festivals

No other type of music is more synonymous with the Caribbean than reggae, and visitors can spend two nights attending reggae concerts hosted by the Moonsplash Reggae Festival. To close out the festival, don't miss out on the raging beach party at Dune Preserve.

Making its debut in November 2016, Livin in the Sun music festival shook things up on Anguilla's Sandy Island. It featured today's most popular hits with a special focus on EDM (electronic dance music). Along with twelve different top artists from around the world, Anguilla's famous local DJ Sugar and Sandy Island's house mixmaster, Yooshe, hosted a multiple day and night music extravegenza that had everyone's body rockin'. Nighttime event tickets are $50(USD) and all-day event tickets are $200(USD).

Other Events and Festivals

In January, the Anguilla Craft Shop hosts the Annual Arts and Crafts Exhibition. Local artists show of their works, and some even put on demonstrations.

Beginning during the last week of January and running into February, Anguilla honors those who protect and serve them during Police Week. Events include a block party, fashion show, and a performance of the police choir.

If natural beauty moves you, stop in to the ABC Annual Flower Show in February . The event is hosted by the Anguilla Beautification Club.

The Festival del Mar in April honors all things that have to do with the sea. Sit in on boat races, fishing competitions, triathlons, culinary competitions, and concerts.

May brings the Anguilla Lit Fest, which gives local writers the opportunity to share their works and experiences as well as learn and discuss their craft with international leaders in the industry through a number of events and panels. This is one of the newest festivals hosted on the island each year, but remains popular for readers, writers, and lovers of language.

Taste of Anguilla is a fundraiser for the Anguilla Culinary Team. The event features Anguilla's most celebrated resturants and has drinks that range from Rum Punches to Mojitos.

Check with your hotel concierge or the newspaper during your time on the island, as more events usually occur.

History of Anguilla

After various historical struggles, Anguilla finally won its independence

Early European explorers could have easily overlooked the island of Anguilla due to its out of the way location. But even if they had, the island would not have been deserted. Amerindians had inhabited the island in some form or another for thousands of years before the first British settlers arrived on Anguilla. This uniquely shaped Caribbean destination boasts a rich history that is similar in many aspects to neighboring islands, but also has a past that makes this beautiful island one-of-a-kind.

Pre-Columbian History

About 4000 years ago, magnificent, lush, tropical rainforests covered Anguilla. Amerindians from South America discovered the island about 3500 years ago, long before Christopher Columbus and other European explorers even set eyes on Anguilla. These indigenous people came to Anguilla in dugout canoes and rafts. They were attracted to Anguilla for its prime fishing among the extensive coral reefs that surround the island. These people of the "Preceramic Period" lived in temporary camps and moved around the island gathering food. The Amerindians called the island Malliouhana, which means "arrow-shaped sea serpent" in their native language.

During the fourth century, the Amerindians that were living on Anguilla were of the Salidoid culture. The Saladoids came from the Orinoco Valley region of Venezuela in South America and were farmers, basket weavers, and pottery makers. The Arawak Indians also lived on Anguilla, and were a peaceful group of farmers and hunters who founded much of their work and day-to-day life on their religious beliefs, which were based on the moon, the sun, and two sacred caverns which they believed to be the birthplace of humans.

The Amerindians that settled on Anguilla were deeply ceremonious. Archaeologists have discovered numerous religious artifacts left by the Amerindians, including evidence of religious ceremonies at Big Springs and the Fountain, the two sacred caverns on the eastern side of the island. The most well preserved ceremonial artifacts in the Eastern

Caribbean are found at The Fountain. Many other artifacts such as conch drinking vessels, shell axes, flint blades, and stone objects also indicate the existence of Amerindians on the island.

European Exploration

Around 1493 Columbus sailed passed Anguilla, but never actually set foot on the island. European explorers changed the island's name to Anguilla, which means "eel," apparently because of its elongated shape. It has been documented that the first European explorers to settle on the island were the Dutch. They are said to have built a fort on Anguilla in 1631, but the remains of the fort have never been found. About twenty years later, British settlers from the neighboring island of St. Kitt's colonized Anguilla. When the Europeans discovered that the soil on Anguilla was rich enough to grow small crops of corn and tobacco, they began to establish plantations. However, the Carib Indians, a warrior people from South America, destroyed the explorers' settlements in 1650. The Caribs had also overtaken the population of Arawak Indians who previously resided on Anguilla.

For the most part, the island remained a crown colony. In 1666 French forces overtook Anguilla, but the island was returned to British rule the following year under the Treaty of Breda. The French made several more attempts to invade the island, but most of their efforts were short-lived, and the British maintained control of Anguilla. The struggle for power between the British and French, which dominated Anguilla's history for about 150 years, took its toll on the island and its economy.

Anguilla also launched some assaults of its own and took over the French half of Martinique in 1744. The Anguillans held control of the island for just a few years until the Treaty of Aix-la-Chapelle returned it to the French in 1748.

Plantation Life

Following in the footsteps of the rest of the Caribbean, Anguilla had a plantation-based economy. Rum, sugar, cotton, indigo, fustic, and mahogany were the island's main exports. But, because of the Anguilla's arid conditions, the plantations on the island were small and could not support the large number of African slaves brought to work the land. Many of the slaves were forced to focus on maintaining self-sustaining food plots, which created a form of independence among the African slaves even before their official emancipation.

The British passed the Emancipation Act in on August 1, 1834, and slavery on the island ended by 1838. Anguilla society became one of peasants who took advantage of the fertile soil. After the end of slavery on Anguilla, economic conditions on the island were harsh for about 70 years, and many people left to find work on neighboring

Caribbean islands. Those that stayed on Anguilla helped to create a population of hardworking and independent people.

British Rule

Because it was difficult for England to rule Anguilla effectively from London, Britain made the island a federation in 1871. But Anguilla was not happy with this arrangement and petitioned British council for direct British rule. Anguilla declared its independence in 1967 when it was granted statehood.

Crime

All About Crime in Anguilla
Anguilla is generally a safe and peaceful island paradise
Although travelers should never fail to be aware of the threat and danger of crime, Anguilla's vacationers will be heartened to learn that island has a relatively low crime rate. Nevertheless, travelers should always take common sense precautions in order to ensure their safety.

Whenever traveling abroad, vacationers should keep a watchful eye on themselves, their possessions, and their surroundings. Although crime is not typically considered a problem on the small peaceful island, Anguilla has seen both petty and violent crimes. If you should fall victim to crime while vacationing in Anguilla, immediately contact the local authorities and your local consulate or embassy. Consular agents will assist you in securing any legal, medical, or financial assistance that you may need as a result of the crime.

Take common sense precautions to protect yourself. Never leave your valuables and possessions unattended at the beach or in your car, as unguarded items are easy targets for thieves. Additionally, never leave your valuables unguarded in your hotel room. Many hotels have in-room safes or a front desk safety deposit in which to lock your important possessions. Passports are popular items for thieves, and travelers should always keep these safe and secure.

Flashing large amounts of money, jewelry, or electronic equipment can increase your risk of falling victim to a theft. Travelers may wish to keep credit cards, cash, and passports in several locations in order to prevent all of their valuables from being stolen in the event of a theft. Other common sense precautions include avoiding deserted and unlit areas at night, especially if you are alone.

Travelers who visit Anguilla should not consider crime a serious concern. Still, it's best to always be on the lookout for the safety of you and your possessions. Although the island's weather and beaches makes Anguilla a tropical paradise, travelers should never let their guard down.

Travel Guide
Accomodation

Anguilla Accomodation Options

Many of Anguilla's accommodations are concentrated along the island's 30 plus beaches

All kind of travelers, from honeymooners and families to international film stars, travel to Anguilla to enjoy the quiet and seclusion of this small, peaceful island. Here you'll find world renowned hotels and resorts along with isolated villas and accommodating inns.

Prospective vacationers have a number of resources for finding the accommodations that best fit their vacation style. If you have your heart set on a particular amenity, look to our Best Hotels For pages, which rank the top hotels and resorts on Anguilla based on specific criteria. If you like the idea of rankings but are more interested in the overall appeal than special sectors, our Star Ratings pages could be just the ticket.

Location

Hotels and resorts in Anguilla are mostly located on the south and north coasts of the island though there are a few on the interior. As you search for information about reserving your hotel room of choice, keep in mind that many web sites that allow you to book your travel on-line will often list hotels as being in a recognizable city, when in fact, the hotel is miles away. It is always best to inquire specifically with the hotel you are considering to ensure it is located where you think it is.

The southern coast, from east to west, consists of Sandy Ground, West End, Rendezvous Bay, and Blowing Point. Each of these cities is populated with a variety of resort, villa, and apartment accommodations, so finding your home-away-from-home will hardly be a struggle.

In the center of Anguilla is The Valley. This is where the central business district is located, so guests traveling on business will want to locate from. Read from Anguilla Hotel Page in this book.

To the north is Shoal Bay and Island Harbour. Shoal Bay and Island Harbour are teeming with hotels, inns, and villas, but as you move to the northeast section of Anguilla you'll discover a remote area of beaches but very few lodgings. Guests who want to experience this side of the island would do well to book a hotel in a larger city and make the commute.

Although accommodations tend to be expensive in Anguilla, travelers can find lodging that caters to smaller budgets. Travelers who wish to enjoy Anguilla at any cost will find world class hotels and rental villas to create an unforgettable vacation experience.

Hotels

Anguilla offers hotel possibilities that will be suitable for almost any type of visitor. Select from glitzy resorts, low-cost accommodations, and plenty more in between. For travelers planning on wining-and-dining quite a bit, you can find a handful of hotels that offer outstanding on-site dining. Read further information on them by clicking on them.

One of the best properties in Anguilla to find on-site dining is CuisinArt Resort & Spa. The resort offers nine different suite options ranging in size and capacity. The resort is fully capable of provided the perfect place for any getaway, whether guests are looking for a small honeymoon escape or large family vacation. You can reach them at (264) 498-2000.

One place along the waterfront worth mentioning is Viceroy Anguilla. Caribbean flare meets elegant decor at Viceroy Anguilla earning this resort a spot on the list of Top 10 Sweet Suites in the Caribbean. The luxury accommodations provided by the resort were custom designed by Kelly Wearstler, and feature Sferra linens, premium appliances and cookware, an espresso machine, wine chiller, warming drawers, and a washer and dryer. Visitors can call them at (264) 497-7000.

Travelers who are in search of good on-site dining possibilities may want to look into Cap Juluca. This renovated facility has blossomed into a truly stunning property, complete with lavish guest rooms, a sprawling library selection, relaxing lounge areas, thousands of delightful flowers and more. This resort takes every measure imaginable to ensure that guests have the most luxurious service. You can call them at (264) 497-6666.

Of course, you'll find a wider range of choices. To navigate to our complete page about hotels on the island, see Anguilla Hotels page in this book.

Condos and Villa Complexes

There are non-hotel lodging options on the island, including a condominium building and several villa complexes. Beach-goers can usually expect to enjoy easy access to the beach, as a lot of the villas and other accommodations are located right on the shore.

If you prefer to stay at a exclusive property, Zemi Beach House Resort & Spa is probably a good place to begin your search. Zemi Beach House Resort & Spa is a six-acre oceanfront resort that takes its guests on an journey of renewal and rest. Zemi Beach is inspired by the ancient healing traditions of the Tanio people and aspires to inspire a deep sense of well being and contentment. If you want to call ahead of time, you can do so at (264) 584-0001.

An excellent option for travelers interested in accommodations in Anguilla is CéBlue Villas & Beach Resort. Offering some of the most luxurious vacation villas on Anguilla, CeBlue Villas was ranked by Fodors as one of the "10 Best New Caribbean Resorts" in 2013. Thanks to the humongous offering of space, beautiful hilltop views, and private crystal plunge pools it is easy to agree that a relaxing getaway doesn't get much better than this. They're located at 1264 Valley road.

Villa Sheriva at Sheriton Estates is another property worth considering. A four-diamond resort which takes the word 'exclusive' to new heights. The accommodations are staggering and chic, from suites to villas, and offer every guest the chance to experience luxury at its utmost. There is also a long list of amenities available to guests of the resort, including several that can't be found elsewhere. If you have questions, call them at (809) 264-4989 ext. 898.

Fortunately, you'll be able to find some other choices. To reach our detailed guide to more villa complexes on the island, from Villa complex page in this book.

Individual Villas

Some often prefer the seclusion offered by one of the many individual rental properties. Readers can get more details about the private rental properties on Anguilla by reading from Villa Rental page in this book.

All-Inclusive Accommodations

Some people enjoy the simplicity of an all-inclusive package. There are many reasons why these packages are so popular. For instance, they offer unparalleled relaxation without the worry of budgeting each day's expenses. The two accommodations below are the only all-inclusive properties available here.

For those wanting to stay somewhere with a lively bar scene, Anguilla Great House Beach Resort is one location you might want to think about. Elegant rooms decorated in a 'Caribbean Gingerbread' style offer spacious rooms that are comfortably equipped with patios for long hours of lounging and relaxation. Amenities come both in-room and beach-side. You can reach them at (264) 497-6061.

For visitors that like to take part in a variety of outdoor pursuits, Ani Villas is one of those spots that provides plenty of opportunities for recreation. Forget about your busy life back home and enter a world unlike any other when you book at stay at Ani Villas. With a staff prepared to handle every single last service you can think of and the possibility of catering to parties of up to 100 people, this is truly a unique destination. If you want to call before you go, you can do so at (501) 226-4270.

Although the term "all-inclusive" implies that you get everything you need in one package, some beverages and amenities may not be covered. Be sure to investigate to confirm what's included in each all-inclusive package.

All-Inclusive Resorts

All-inclusive resorts are not typical on the small island of Anguilla

Travelers who make the trip to Anguilla may be able to mix with international celebrities who escape to the island to get out of the limelight. While there are many luxury properties, all-inclusive resorts are hard to come by, but that doesn't mean that they don't exist.

Vacationers who choose to stay at any of the island's fine resorts can typically choose from a number of vacation packages or meal plans to make their time in Anguilla an experience specified directly to their needs and wants. Travelers can choose from theme oriented vacation packages that cater to a certain type of experience. Spa packages will include daily treatments, allowing vacationers to relax with massages and aromatherapy. Other resorts may offer wedding and honeymoon packages that include champagne, flowers, sunset cruises, couples massages, and more. Since some of the island's finest restaurants are located at these luxury resorts, some vacation packages cater to food lovers. Many hotels have meal plans for an additional daily fee per person that can include either all three meals or only breakfast and lunch. Luxury hotels generally offer a variety of complimentary services that are included in the room rate, including non-motorized water sports, fitness facilities, and a continental breakfast.

Critics of all-inclusive vacation packages suggest that they prevent travelers from experiencing other parts of the island. Although Anguilla does not have a great number of shopping sites and popular tourist attractions, travelers should certainly not confine their vacation to a single hotel and beach. There are a number of stunning beaches and intimate offshore islands that should not be missed. Some all-inclusive packages may include the use of a rental car for a short period of time, and travelers should seize the opportunity to explore the island. Prices for four-night packages can begin as low as $799(USD), and continue to increase as benefits and nights are added. Some seven-night stays can cost more than $10,000(USD).

Anguilla Great House Beach Resort is one of the few hotels on the island that can be classified as all-inclusive. Anguilla Great House is located on Anguilla's West End on Rendezvous Bay. The property consists of 27 cottages trimmed with bright shutters. Guests not only enjoy beautiful views of the Caribbean Sea from their cottages, but the landscape of nearby St. Martin appears in the distance. Included in the all-inclusive price of about $95(USD) per person, per night ($50(USD) for those under the age of six), is the use of snorkel gear and other non-motorized watersports equipment, transportation to the ferry terminal or airport at the conclusion of your stay, and three meals a day. These rates are based upon double occupancy, and require a minimum of five nights stay. Otherwise, guests may choose to pay a regular room rate, and possibly add on a meal plan to their deal.

Those who shy away from large, commercial resort complexes will feel at-home at most of Anguilla's lodgings. Here, prestigious resorts that value privacy and luxury offer meal plans and other options to travelers looking for a more laid-back vacation experience.

Listed below are two of Anguilla's all-inclusives. Click on each to compare their dining options, activities and amenities. Maybe one of them is perfect for you.

Eco Tourism Accommodations

Travelers can explore Anguilla's natural beauty while the sun is out

Although Anguilla is small, and rugged in places, the island's terrain is suitable for hiking and biking. There are also countless opportunities for watersports and adventures. While travelers have several options for eco-tourism activities, campsites are not to be found on the island.

Travelers seeking campgrounds and large swaths of rainforests to explore should consider visiting another Caribbean island. Neither the beaches nor the island's interior have any official campgrounds.

Immigration officers will ask travelers for the address of their resort or rental property upon arrival to the island.

Although Anguilla is not a popular eco-tourism site, vacationers can indulge in mountain biking and hiking along trails in the island's interior, or take a horseback ride along the beach. Birdwatchers can look for more than 100 bird species on the island. The Anguilla National Trust was established in 1993 to oversee the protection of natural resources and land, and has undertaken projects such as the restoration of beach dunes.

Eco-tourism activities can also be enjoyed in the water. Take a glass bottom boat to enjoy the underwater scenery. For an even closer look, enjoy snorkeling on one of the island's 33 beaches. Several excellent scuba dive sites are located along the northeast coast.

Although vacationers may come to Anguilla primarily to relax on beaches such as Shoal Bay, active travelers can indulge in several eco-tourism activities to get a sense of the local flora and fauna. Read more about nature in Anguilla by reading Anguilla Attraction page in this book.

Hotels

Detailed information about hotels in Anguilla

The government of Anguilla limits commercial development on the island. You won't find big, international all-inclusive resorts with casinos and other large scale amenities here. Nevertheless, hotels and resorts in Anguilla are among the nicest in the Caribbean.

A large number of the hotels in Anguilla are located in the popular southwest and northeast areas of the island, home to some of the most inviting and captivating beaches in the Caribbean. While a few of the island's resorts will have about 100 rooms, many will have 20 or fewer, giving travelers additional privacy and intimacy.

Rates

Anguilla can be quite an expensive destination, although travelers can find reasonable rates and accommodations, especially outside of the peak winter holiday season. Holiday season rates can start as low as $90(USD) to $120(USD), but will quickly climb up to $245(USD) and continue to rise above $1,000(USD) a night. The most expensive suites and hotel villas cost between $3,000(USD) and $6,450(USD). Most room rates are based on double occupancy. Suite rates may be based on a relevant occupancy limit. Traveling in the off season will save travelers considerable amounts of money, but some hotels may close during the months of September and October.

Looking for an Anguillan hotel that's perfect for the whole family? Our guide allows you to browse properties that are best for family vacations—even those with the most swimming pools.

Hotels On Anguilla

Anguilla offers hotel possibilities that will be suitable for nearly every kind of visitor. Find budget hotels, luxury resorts, and plenty more in between. For those who plan on soaking up a few rays by the pool, there are a few properties to pick from with great swimming facilities. Read more details on each property by clicking the names.

One of the best properties in Anguilla to find a variety of on-site dining possibilities is Cap Juluca. This facility has blossomed into a truly stunning property, complete with lavish guest rooms, a sprawling library selection, relaxing lounge areas, thousands of delightful flowers and more. This resort ensures that guests have luxurious service. If you want to know more, call them at (264) 497-6666.

A interesting property along the coast that you could consider is Malliouhana, an Auberge Resort. A high luxury hotel inspired by classic Mediterranean décor, this hotel and spa sits atop a high bluff overlooking the beaches and Caribbean Sea below. If you are looking to call ahead of time, you can do so at (877) 733-3611.

For those seeking to stay somewhere with an active bar scene, Anacaona Boutique Hotel is one destination you might want to think about. An affordable alternative to the ritzier hotels on the island, Anacaona Boutique Hotel mixes genuine hospitality with a stunning location to allow for the perfect blend of sophistication and fun for your island retreat. The hotel is owned and operated by a Swiss couple who pay close attention to each individual's needs, and a variety of guestrooms evoke the Caribbean in architecture, décor, and space. If you have questions, call them at (264) 497-6827.

The following table lists more details regarding the 25 available hotels.

HOTELS ON ANGUILLA				
Name	Type	Phone Number	Star Rating	Location
Allamanda Beach Club	Hotel	(264) 497-5217		3.3 mi. Northeast of Central the Valley
Anacaona Boutique Hotel	Hotel	(264) 497-6827		0.4 mi. South West of Central Meads Bay
Anguilla Great House Beach Resort	Resort	(264) 497-6061		1.2 mi. West of Central Blowing Point
Arawak Beach Inn	Hotel	(264) 497-4888		1.8 mi. North of Central East End
Cap Juluca	Resort	(264) 497-6666		1.1 mi. South of Central Meads Bay
Carimar Beach Club	Hotel	(264) 497-6881		0.4 mi. Northeast of Central Meads Bay
Covecastles Resort	Hotel	(264) 497-6801		1.9 mi. South West of Central Meads Bay
CuisinArt Resort & Spa	Resort	(264) 498-2000		1.5 mi. West of Central Blowing Point
Ferryboat Inn	Hotel	(264) 497-6613		0.5 mi. South-Southwest of Central Blowing Point

Frangipani Beach Resort	Resort	--		0.2 mi. South West of Central Meads Bay
Ku Hotel	Hotel	(809) 264-4972 ext. 011		3.1 mi. North-Northeast of Central the Valley
La Vue Boutique Inn	Hotel	(264) 497-6623		1.2 mi. North of Central Blowing Point
Las Esquinas	B & B	--		1.5 mi. East-Northeast of Central Blowing Point
Lloyd's Bed and Breakfast	B & B	(264) 497-2351		Crocus Hill, Central Anguilla
Malliouhana, an Auberge Resort	Hotel	(877) 733-3611		0.5 mi. North-Northeast of Central Meads Bay
Mariners Cliffside Beach Resort	Cottages	--		1.2 mi. North of Central Blowing Point
Nathan's Cove	Hotel	--		0.2 mi. Northeast of Central Meads Bay
Paradise Cove Resort	Hotel	(264) 497-6603		0.9 mi. Southeast of Central Meads Bay
Quintessence Hotel	Hotel	(800) 234-7468		1.9 mi. West-Northwest of Central Blowing Point
Rendezvous Bay Hotel & Villas	Hotel	(264) 584-6501		0.8 mi. West of Central Blowing Point
Serenity Cottages	Cottages	--		3.3 mi. Northeast of Central the Valley
The Manoah	Hotel	(264) 498-		3.4 mi. Northeast of

		5900	Central the Valley
The Reef	Hotel	--	1.4 mi. West of Central Blowing Point
Turtle's Nest Beach Resort	Hotel	(264) 462-6378	0.1 mi. South West of Central Meads Bay
Viceroy Anguilla	Hotel	(264) 497-7000	0.6 mi. West-Southwest of Central Meads Bay

Of course, you will find some other property types you can find. To read our complete guide to other kinds of accommodations available for Anguilla, Read on Accommodation page in this book.

Villa Complexes

Rental properties are popular options for travelers in Anguilla

Rental condos, villas, and apartments in Anguilla allow travelers to unwind in innovative spaces amongst luxurious decors and amenities. Guests can enjoy privacy and comfort without the crowd of a resort.

The island of Anguilla is so alluring due to its natural beauty, its quiet atmosphere, and the seclusion that it offers compared to other Caribbean islands. There are no direct flights to the island, so travelers must take extra steps to reach this small paradise. Unlike neighboring Sint Maarten, there are no casinos and no grand, duty-free shopping complexes. Discerning travelers who choose to make Anguilla their destination typically desire a luxurious retreat in beautiful surroundings and are willing to pay the premium prices that come with such things.

Because rental properties can be luxurious, they often come at a high price. Small apartments and rentals can run as low as $80(USD) to $100(USD), but rates of around $250(USD) to $650(USD) are more typical. High-end villas and rental properties can cost travelers from $850(USD) to $6,450(USD) per night. Weekly rates can soar up to $35,000(USD).

Rental properties, discretely nestled along glowing strips of Anguilla's white sand, provide travelers with the ultimate in comfort and privacy. Travelers who choose these types of accommodations have the freedom and autonomy to choose when they eat, sleep, and relax. Rather than worrying about reservations and dining times, travelers can use their kitchens to prepare meals. Although the island has a number of internationally renowned restaurants that serve mouthwatering cuisine, occasionally cooking meals in the privacy of a rental villa can be both cost-friendly and romantic.

Condos and Villa Complexes On Anguilla

You'll be able to find non-standard hotel accommodation options on the island, which include a condominium building and a large variety of villa complexes. Beach-goers can generally expect to find easy access to the beach, as many villas and other accommodations are situated right on the water. Read additional info for them by clicking on their names.

Guests hoping to book their stay in Anguilla will enjoy properties like **Villa Sheriva at Sheriton Estates**. A four-diamond resort which takes the word 'exclusive' to new heights. The accommodations are staggering and chic, from suites to villas, and offer every guest the chance to experience luxury at its utmost. There is also a long list of amenities available to guests of the resort, including several that can't be found elsewhere. If you want to call ahead of time, do so at (809) 264-4989 ext. 898.

A interesting property on the waterfront that you could consider is Altamer Villas. Altamer Villas are contemporary dwellings in Anguilla that welcome hip vacationers with an eye for design. The villas are located on a private island setting, feature contemporary architecture, rare art, and modern amenities. To contact them, call (264) 498-4000.

Another good choice to consider available is Shoal Bay Villas. This quaint resort features rooms available in studio, one, and two-bedroom apartments, all with a kitchen. Optional views accompany the room selection. Visitors can reach them at (264) 497-2051.

Additional information about the several condo and villa complex possibilities are summarized directly below.

CONDOS AND VILLA COMPLEXES ON ANGUILLA

Name	Phone Number	Star Rating	Location
Altamer Villas	(264) 498-4000		1.6 mi. South West of Central Meads Bay
Ani Villas	(501) 226-4270		Central Anguilla
Arbon Villas	(978) 369-2546		1.0 mi. South West of Central Meads Bay
Beach Houses at Covecastles	(264) 497-6801		1.9 mi. South West of Central Meads Bay
Blue Waters Apartments	--		1.6 mi. South West of Central Meads Bay
Callaloo Club Villas	(264) 498-8600		0.9 mi. South West of Central Blowing Point
CéBlue Villas & Beach Resort	(264) 462-1000		The Valley, Central Anguilla
Indigo Reef	(264) 497-6144		1.6 mi. West-Southwest of Central Meads Bay
Kamique Villas	(264) 497-6049		1.3 mi. East-Northeast of Central Blowing Point
La Residence	--		1.3 mi. North of Central Blowing Point
Maria Villa	(264) 497-2427		Sandy Ground Village, Central Anguilla

Meads Bay Beach Villas	(264) 497-0271		0.1 mi. West of Central Meads Bay
Patsy's Seaside Villas	--		0.4 mi. South of Central Blowing Point
Shoal Bay Villas	(264) 497-2051		3.2 mi. North-Northeast of Central the Valley
Sur La Plage	--		0.4 mi. West-Southwest of Central Meads Bay
Twin Palms Villas	(264) 498-2741		0.4 mi. Northeast of Central Meads Bay
Villa Sheriva at Sheriton Estates	(809) 264-4989 ext. 898		0.8 mi. South-Southwest of Central Meads Bay
Villas at Long Bay	(264) 497-6049		0.9 mi. Northeast of Central Meads Bay
Zemi Beach House Resort & Spa	(264) 584-0001		2.8 mi. North-Northeast of Central the Valley

If you want to learn about a wider selection of places beyond what's offered here, you might want to find others. To read more about other kinds of accommodations for Anguilla, Read on Accommodation page in this book.

Villa Rentals

Anguilla Individual Villa Rentals

Individual Villas

Single rental properties also tend to be very popular on Anguilla. You'll find plenty of choices for unique villa styles and feels. Take a minute to read the following table if you want more information.

INDIVIDUAL VILLAS ON ANGUILLA

Name	Phone Number	Bedrooms	Bathrooms	Location
Alcyon Villa	--	5	4	0.8 mi. South of Central East End
Alegria Villa	--	4	4	0.6 mi. South-Southwest of Central Blowing Point
Ambrosia Villa	--	7	10	2.1 mi. Northwest of Central East End
Anguilla Sunset Beach House	(954) 634-7548	4	4	1.8 mi. North-Northwest of Central the Valley
Animos Villa	--	5	5	1.8 mi. West of Central Blowing Point
Argianno Villa	--	4	4	1.0 mi. East of Central Blowing Point
Azure Villa	--	--	--	2.4 mi. North of Central Sandy Hill Bay
Azure Villa	--	5	4	2.0 mi. Northwest of Central East End

BP Villa	--	4	4	2.8 mi. North-Northeast of Central the Valley
Balihai Villa	--	2	2	0.5 mi. Southeast of Central Blowing Point
Banana Wind Villas	(510) 315-0550	--	--	0.9 mi. East of Central Blowing Point
Beach Court Villa	--	8	8	2.8 mi. North-Northeast of Central the Valley
Beach Escape Villa	--	5	5	0.5 mi. South-Southwest of Central Blowing Point
Beaches Edge Villa	--	4	5	0.6 mi. Southeast of Central Blowing Point
Bird of Paradise Villa	--	4	4	1.0 mi. South West of Central East End
Black Pearl	--	4	4	3.2 mi. North-Northeast of Central the Valley
Coconut Palm Villa	--	3	3	0.4 mi. Northeast of Central Meads Bay
Coyaba Villa	--	6	6	0.9 mi. East of Central Blowing Point
Desert Rose Villa	--	4	4	2.0 mi. North of Central East End
Emerald Reef Villa	--	5	4	0.8 mi. South-Southwest of Central East End
Fletch's Cove	(610) 420-	1	2	2.5 mi. South West of

	4753			Central the Valley
Gardenia Villa	--	5	5	0.7 mi. South-Southwest of Central East End
Imperial Villa	(863) 968-6729	4	4	1.2 mi. North of Central Blowing Point
Indigo Villa	--	9	9	2.4 mi. South West of Central the Valley
Jasmine Villa	--	2	2	0.4 mi. Northeast of Central Meads Bay
Kishti Villa	--	4	4	1.8 mi. North-Northwest of Central the Valley
L'Embellie Villa	--	3	3	1.5 mi. South of Central the Valley
Le Bleu Villa	--	10	10	2.3 mi. South West of Central the Valley
Les Alize	--	4	4	1.1 mi. West-Southwest of Central Meads Bay
Little Butterfly	(264) 497-3666	1	1	George Hill, Central Anguilla
Little Palm Villa	--	2	2	1.9 mi. North-Northwest of Central East End
Modena Villa	--	5	6	0.6 mi. South-Southeast of Central Meads Bay
Moonraker Villa	--	7	6	0.9 mi. East of Central East End

Moonrise Villa	--	3	3	1.9 mi. South-Southwest of Central the Valley
Mystique Villa	--	6	8	0.8 mi. South of Central Meads Bay
Nirvana	--	4	4	Sandy Ground Village, Central Anguilla
Ocean Crest Villa	--	5	4	0.5 mi. Southeast of Central Blowing Point
Oserian Villa	--	3	3	2.0 mi. South-Southwest of Central the Valley
Panarea Villa	--	3	3	1.1 mi. South West of Central Meads Bay
Papilon	(264) 497-3666	4	4	George Hill, Central Anguilla
Paradise Villa	--	--	--	0.6 mi. South West of Central Blowing Point
Pinnacle Villa	(863) 968-6729	3	3	1.2 mi. North of Central Blowing Point
Rum Punch Villa	--	4	4	1.9 mi. South West of Central East End
Sand Castle Villa	--	4	4	Central Anguilla
Sandcastle Pointe At Shoal Bay	--	4	4	2.6 mi. North of Central the Valley
Seabird Villa	--	4	4	1.1 mi. West of Central Blowing Point

Shutters on the Beach	--	6	5	0.5 mi. South-Southwest of Central Blowing Point
Soleil Villa	--	3	3	1.1 mi. South West of Central Meads Bay
Spyglass Hill Villa	--	4	4	Sandy Ground Village, Central Anguilla
Sweet Return Villa	--	3	3	1.8 mi. Northwest of Central Blowing Point
Tamarind Villa	--	5	5	1.9 mi. Northwest of Central East End
Tequila Sunrise Villa	(239) 344-7810	3	3	2.5 mi. East of Central the Valley
Tortue Villa	--	--	--	2.4 mi. North of Central Sandy Hill Bay
Tranquil Tides Villa	--	4	5	2.6 mi. North-Northeast of Central the Valley
Tranquility Villa	--	2	2	2.4 mi. Northwest of Central East End
Ultimacy Villa	--	8	11	2.0 mi. North-Northwest of Central East End
Villa Amarilla	--	5	5	2.0 mi. North-Northwest of Central East End
Villa Harmony	--	8	9	0.8 mi. South of Central Meads Bay
Villa Infinity	--	7	8	0.8 mi. South of Central

				Meads Bay
Waters Edge Villa	--	5	5	0.5 mi. Southeast of Central Blowing Point
Wesley House	--	3	3	1.5 mi. North of Central East End
White Cedars Villa	--	3	3	2.0 mi. East of Central the Valley
Zebra Villa	--	2	2	0.4 mi. Northeast of Central Meads Bay
Zenaida Beach & Tennis Estate	--	7	7	0.8 mi. South West of Central East End

If you are looking for a wider range of properties beyond the category here, you should look at other locations when read on Read on Accommodation page in this book.

Activities

Sports, shopping, and cultural showcases are all popular activities in Anguilla

The great thing about planning a trip to Anguilla is that the island is both laid back and active at once. Those who prefer to spend their days quietly sailing or on the beach will find what they are looking for, as will the vacationer who is always on the go, seeking out the best shopping deals and the most happening nightlife.

Bike and Scooter Rental

If you like the idea of exploring a new environment with the wind in your face, there's a place that can help you. To visit our page about bike or scooter rentals, read on our Bike and Mopeds page in this book

Diving

You'll find several dive operators and at least 16 different dive sites to choose from. To navigate to our page about scuba diving in this area, , read on our Diving page in this book.

Events and Festivals

Depending on when you plan to visit, you might have an opportunity to attend a music festival or other scheduled event. The Summer Festival, which takes place in July and August, is one of the best displays of Anguillian culture; while music lovers will want to be present for the Moonsplash Annual Music Festival in March. , read on our Event and Festival page in this book to learn more about interesting events that might be taking place during your vacation.

Fishing

If there are some experienced anglers in your group, they're in luck -- 10 charter fishing services operate from this area. Make your way to Fishing page which is all about fishing in the area if you'd like to discover more details.

Golf

Like to play golf? Anguilla isn't exactly paved with golf greens from end to end, but there's one course to be aware of. The only course in the area is Cuisin Art Resort Golf Course. Furthermore, you can visit read on Caribbean Golf through Caribbean book if you'd like to learn additional facts about golfing throughout the Caribbean.

Sailing and Boating

The table just below offers some details on area firms that will enable you to spend some time out on the open water.

BOATING OPPORTUNITIES ON ANGUILLA

Name	Phone	Location

Calypso Charters	(246) 584-8504	0.4 mi. South of Central Blowing Point
Garfield's Sea Tours - Gotcha!	(264) 497-2956	Sandy Ground Village, Central Anguilla
Junior's Glass Bottom Boat	(264) 235-1008	2.9 mi. North-Northeast of Central the Valley
Sail Chocolat	(264) 497-3394	The Valley, Central Anguilla
Sea Pro Charters	(264) 584-0074	Sandy Ground Village, Central Anguilla

If you're interested in reading about marinas and charter operators read on Sailing and Boating page in this book.

Shopping

Many shoppers associate shopping in the Caribbean with great bargains. Unfortunately, this is not the case in Anguilla. In fact, many visitors find clothing, jewelry, and other items to be overpriced. You'll find your money is best spent on locally hand made crafts and artwork; even if they are expensive, at least they are unique.

If there are some folks who enjoy window shopping in your group, they might be interested to know that there are more than 52 retail stores to browse in this area. Navigate to Shopping page in this book if you want to know more about shopping on Anguilla.

Sightseeing

Sightseeing is also a good way to use some of your time in Anguilla. Among other sights, the area has 4 historic sites and various other attractions of interest to visitors, read on Attraction page in this book to see our article about area sightseeing and attractions.

Details concerning a firm that can help you enjoy some local sightseeing can be found in the following table:

SIGHTSEEING SERVICES ON ANGUILLA

Name	Type	Phone	Location
Anguilla National Trust	Travel and Tour Operators	(264) 497-5054	The Valley, Central Anguilla
Anguilla Watersports Stand Up Paddleboard Tours	Travel and Tour Operators	(264) 584-1204	Anguilla
Malliouhana Travel & Tours Ltd	Travel and Tour Operators	(264) 497-2431	Stoney Ground, Central Anguilla
Nature Explorers Anguilla	Nature Tourism Service	(264) 584-0346	The Valley, Central Anguilla
Seagrape Eco Tours	Excursions and Sightseeing Service	(721) 586-0297	Anguilla

Snorkeling

If you enjoy snorkeling you'll be pleased to know you'll have plenty of chances to do so along the coast of Anguilla. Follow this link to view our page regarding local snorkeling opportunities.

Spas

Relaxing for a few hours in a spa just might be the highlight of your entire vacation. It shouldn't be hard to find a spa you like, considering that there are 8 spas located in this area. Visit "Spas" page in this book concerning spas in the area if you want to get additional specifics.

Sports

A vacation in the Caribbean just isn't the same without time spent by the seaside. Instead of just parking your self in the sand of one of Anguilla's 33 beaches, you could decide to take a more active approach, and go swimming in the pool at your hotel, or in the beautiful, calm waters that surround the island.

If you want to stay active during your Anguilla vacation, but prefer to do it on dry land, there are plenty of other options available. Some hotels offer gymnasiums, as well as tennis, basketball, and beach volleyball courts. You can also choose to go jogging, or explore the island on foot by walking along the beaches or exploring a hiking trail. American sports fans can also enjoy an relatively unfamiliar spectator sport when they visit Anguilla: Cricket. Anguillians love cricket, and take it very seriously. Check game schedules while you are on the island and you may be able to catch a game at Ronald Webster Park.

Tennis

If you want to play some tennis your best bet is to stay at a hotel with a tennis court. Fortunately, you can choose from 4 properties in the area that offer tennis.

The following list can help with your decision making process. At a glance, you'll see the number of courts on-site, whether lights are available for evening play, and some other details. Click on the names to learn more about the property.

ACCOMMODATIONS WITH TENNIS ON ANGUILLA				
Property	Location	Tennis Courts	Lit Courts	Tennis Pro
Cap Juluca	1.1 mi. South of Central Meads Bay	3		
Malliouhana, an Auberge Resort	0.5 mi. North-Northeast of Central Meads Bay	2		
Carimar Beach Club	0.4 mi. Northeast of Central Meads Bay	--		
Mariners Cliffside Beach Resort	1.2 mi. North of Central Blowing Point	2		

For instance, Cap Juluca has a tennis pro who can give you lessons or tips for improving your game.

Other Activities

Information about lots of other activities are provided in the following chart.

OTHER ACTIVITIES ON ANGUILLA

Name	Type	Phone	Location
Anguilla Tennis Academy	Tennis Club	(264) 498-0697	0.4 mi. North of Central Blowing Point
Anguilla Watersports	Watersports Operator	(264) 584-1204	0.9 mi. South of Central Meads Bay
Dolphin Discovery	Dolphin Encounter Service	(866) 393-5158	0.5 mi. South of Central Blowing Point
Dungeon Gym	Fitness Centers and Instructors	(264)476-061	1.2 mi. Northwest of Central Blowing Point
Freedom Rentals Watersports	Watersports Operator	(264) 498-2830	North Hill Village, Central Anguilla
Seaside Stables Anguilla	Horseback Riding Site	(264) 235-3667	0.8 mi. Southeast of Central Meads Bay
The Anguilla Aqua Park	Watersports Operator	(264) 584-1204	0.9 mi. Southeast of Central Meads Bay
Tropical Paradise	Watersports Operator	(264) 584-1201	0.9 mi. Southeast of Central Meads Bay

Anguilla is a quiet island with more to do than any vacationer might expect. Whether you spend your days shopping, hiking, or out on the water, your Anguilla vacation can be as laid back or action packed as you want it to be.

Bikes & Mopeds

Renting a Bike or Scooter in Anguilla

Take the road less traveled by renting a moped or bike while on vacation

Renting a bike or moped is a wonderful way to sightsee and get around the island of Anguilla. These two-wheeled vehicles give you the freedom to travel when you want, without the expense and hassle of renting a car.

Anguilla is covered in gorgeous natural beauty and superb tropical scenery, so why be limited to just the areas that you can reach by car. One of the best ways to experience the island's intriguing outdoors is to traverse the island by bike or moped. As an alternative to driving or public transportation, bikes and mopeds allow you to break the constraints of traditional transportation by leaving the city limits and crowded streets far behind.

Anguilla's miles of bike trails are a great way to get some fresh air and are the perfect way to see the island's more remote spots, like its beautiful rainforests. Many hotels offer weekly bike rentals at special discounted rates for their guests.

Mopeds are a convenient way to travel through the city streets. With gas prices at an all time high, vacationers may want to consider renting a moped. These motorized two-wheel vehicles get much better mileage than than their four-wheeled counterparts. Renting a moped or bike is also considerably cheaper than renting a car. Bikes start at about $10(USD) per day, and scooters start around $27(USD) per day, which is a fraction of the cost of renting a car. As always, use caution when navigating a moped or bike on Anguilla's roads.

If you are intrigued by the idea of feeling the wind on your face as you move along, you're in luck -- there is an agency that can help make it happen.

If you're ready to make a reservation, you should consider Freedom Rentals ATV Tours. You may explore both land and sea with the 4 wheel ATV bikes and 2 seated motorboats, making for an exciting adventure! They are situated in Blowing Point, in southwestern Anguilla.

The chart just below shows more details regarding the one rental service we know of that operates in this area.

Bike And Moped Rental On Anguilla				
Name	Type	Phone	Location	Island
Freedom Rentals ATV Tours	Bicycle, Moped or ATV Rental Service	(264) 498-2830	Blowing Point, Southwestern part of Anguilla	Anguilla

Strap on your helmet and get ready for the ride of your life on the exciting tropical island of Anguilla!

Diving

Scuba Diving Near Anguilla

A handful of marine parks and some good dive sites make up the underwater splendors of Anguilla

Anguilla is considered to be a great Caribbean locale to visit if you are looking to escape the fast paced, crowded, big-city life. To further get away, try exploring a whole new world; a world where it is quiet and calm, where you can go at your own pace and experience no interruptions.

This world, of course, is below the surface of the Caribbean Sea off the coast of Anguilla, which you can explore by diving and snorkeling.

The waters surrounding Anguilla range in visibility from 60 to 100 ft below the surface, and tend to stay around 80 degrees Fahrenheit. Divers can expect to see a number of tropical marine animals on their underwater trips, including turtles, Tarpon, eels, and Spotted Eagle Rays.

Choosing the Right Activity for You

Scuba, which is an acronym for "self contained underwater breathing apparatus," allows the participant to delve deeper into the sea by utilizing an air tank in order to stay submerged for an extended period of time. Scuba diving does take some training, and many of Anguilla's resorts offer scuba classes as one of their amenities. If your hotel does not offer these classes, there are numerous dive shops on the island that cater to new scuba divers.

Those that are looking for an underwater activity with less requirements may want to look into snorkeling.

You'll find several dive operators and at least 16 good dive sites in the area.

Dive Operators

If you're looking forward to diving, you might want to check with Anguillan Divers. PADI training takes place in a fresh water pool, and once certified you can move to the sea for wreck, cave, and reef dives. Dive trips leave from Cove Bay every morning at 8:30 a.m. They are located in Meads Bay, in western Anguilla.

A second option is Vigilant Divers. In order to provide optimal training, only four guests are brought out on each boat. You can sign up for a number of different safety courses and tours depending upon your skill level. You can call them at (264) 235-4096.

A third good option is Shoal Bay Scuba. Shoal Bay Scuba is a full service organization, offering everything from PADI certification courses to week-long dive adventures and even equipment rentals. The staff is full certified to help you learn and grow as well as safely complete all of the scuba diving tasks you desire. They're located in Shoal Bay East, in northern Anguilla.

Some information regarding the area's dive services are provided in the chart below.

DIVE OPERATORS NEAR ANGUILLA		
Name	Phone	Location
Anguillan Divers	(264) 497-4750	0.3 mi. Northwest of Central Meads Bay
Shoal Bay Scuba	(264) 235-1482	3.2 mi. North-Northeast of Central the Valley
Vigilant Divers	(264) 235-4096	The Valley, Central Anguilla

Dive Services

Be sure to look at the chart below for an indication of what typical dive services cost in this area.

DIVE SERVICES		
Offering Type	Low Rate	High Rate
Discover Scuba	$ 85.0	$ 120.0
Double Tank Dive	$ 85.0	$ 120.0
Night Dive	$ 50.0	$ 90.0
Open Water Certification	$ 375.0	$ 390.0
Single Tank Dive	$ 50.0	$ 65.0

Dive Sites

Review the chart below to see details concerning some of the area's major dive sites.

Dive Sites Near Anguilla					
Name	Quality	Experience	Max Depth	Latitude	Longitude
Angel Reef	Good	--	65.0	18.2642333333	-63.0254333333
Beacon	Good	--	69.9	18.2482666667	-63.0511
Captain Turtle	Good	--	65.0	18.2488333333	-63.0500166667
Crystal Reef	--	--	--	18.25265	-63.04
Frenchman's Reef	Good	Open Water / CMAS *	100.1	18.2503166667	-63.0470333333
Lobster Reef	Good	--	100.1	18.2667666667	-63.0351666667
MV Catheley H Wreck	Good	--	60.0	18.21045	-63.0935333333
MV Commerce	Good	Open Water / CMAS *	82.0	18.2459833333	-63.0802333333
MV Ida Maria Wreck	Good	Open Water / CMAS *	60.0	18.22215	-63.13765
MV Oosterdiep	Excellent	--	82.0	18.1983666667	-63.1406666667
MV Sarah	Very	Open Water	85.0	18.2525	-

	Good	/ CMAS *			63.1344833333
No Name Reef	Very Good	--	55.1	18.2144333333	- 63.1171166667
Prickly Pear	Fair	--	55.8	18.2616333333	- 63.1750333333
Sea Fan	Good	--	40.0	18.2564166667	- 63.0318166667
Shoal Bay Reef	Good	--	85.0	18.25745	- 63.0354333333
The Garden	Very Good	Open Water / CMAS *	111.9	18.2490333333	- 63.0918166667

To learn more about diving, including suggestions and helpful tips for both beginners and experienced divers, check out this detailed Caribbean scuba diving article.

Tips

> Be aware of currents and stay watchful of your location. Getting too far off course can make returning difficult.

> Wear a watch so you don't lose track of time.

> Do not feed the fish.

> Do not touch the animals or coral. Their protective layers can be stripped away.

- ➤ Never stand or walk on a reef, and tread carefully in shallow water around reefs. (Shuffle your feet to avoid stingrays, and watch out for sea urchin spines.)

- ➤ Never wear jewelry. Caribbean fish, barracudas especially, seem to be drawn to shiny objects that look like their natural prey, small silver fish.

- ➤ Avoid jellyfish, fire coral, and other stinging creatures.

- ➤ Never reach into holes or crevices; animals - especially moray eels - like to make their homes in them.

- ➤ Shark spottings are rare, and sharks that are spotted are usually passive. If you do see a shark, stay calm, and if necessary, move slowly out of the water.

- ➤ Never remove anything from dive sites and reefs; it is illegal to do so.

Anguilla appears to be a sleepy island upon first glance, but in actuality it is alive with beautiful marine life just waiting to be discovered. Plan to make a day of snorkeling or diving, and bring home memories that will last you a lifetime.

Fishing

Fishing Near Anguilla

A little extra legwork is required to plan a fishing or sailing trip in Anguilla

As you sit on one of Anguilla's beaches, staring out at the sea with it's waters bluer than any you've ever seen before, you may find yourself yearning to get a closer look. A day spent fishing is a great way to give into this urge.

Fishing

Fishing in Anguilla tends to be a commercial affair, and sport fishing in Anguilla is still in its infancy. Still, if you'd like nothing more than to drop a line in Anguilla, it is a possibility. While some fishing charter services provide their guests with equipment, this is not true of all of them. If you are an avid angler with an agenda, you may want to consider bringing your own supplies. You can drop a line in shallow waters off of one of the island's beaches or head out to deeper waters so long as you first purchase a permit from the Department of Fisheries and Marine Services. The cost is $30(USD) or $80(ECD). Note that even with a permit, spearfishing is always illegal, and lobster trapping is illegal as well. There are several fishing charters willing to take visitors out a little deeper, and commercial fishermen will sometimes take you out with them for a fee. Both options can be more expensive than elsewhere in the Caribbean, but this is in part due to that fact that they will typically handle obtaining all of your permits for you.

Fly-fisherman can expect to reel in lady fish and snook, while deep sea anglers have been known to catch barracuda, dorado, grouper, kingfish, marlin, sailfish, and wahoo.

Fishing Charters

If you are thinking about deep sea fishing on your vacation, you will find 10 different charter fishing operators that can take you to the best fishing spots.

If you're ready to organize a fishing trip, you can check with Junior's Glass Bottom Boat. For one of the most unique sailing and fishing experiences around, sign up for a sea tour with Junior and his glass bottom boat. Junior has 20 years of experience and knows all of the best sites around the island. They are located in Shoal Bay East, in northern Anguilla.

Another good option is Nature Boy Charters. If you're intrigued by what lies beneath the surface of the sea that surrounds Anguilla, make sure to get in touch with Nature Boy Boat Charters during your stay. They offer numerous marine-inspired services, including sailing, fishing, and snorkeling. You can reach them at (264) 729-5587.

A third option is Gotcha Garfield's Sea Tours. Charters are available by the hour, for half a day, or for a full day. They're found within North Hill Village, in central Anguilla.

The table below provides quick access to a few details regarding fishing charters operating in this area.

Fishing Charters On Anguilla		
Name	Phone	Location
Bevis Rogers	(264) 497-4487	1.7 mi. North of Central East End
Calypso Charter's Fishing	(264) 584-8504	Southwestern part of Anguilla
Ed Carty	(264) 497-2337	Sandy Ground Village, Central Anguilla
Gotcha Garfield's Sea Tours	(264) 235-7902	North Hill Village, Central Anguilla
JR's Glass Bottom Boat Fishing	(264) 235-1008	Anguilla
Junior's Glass Bottom Boat	(264) 497-4456	2.9 mi. North-Northeast of Central the Valley
Nature Boy Charters	(264) 729-5587	2.9 mi. North-Northeast of Central the Valley
No Mercy	(264) 235-6283	Sandy Ground Village, Central Anguilla
Sea Pro Charters Fishing	(264) 584-0074	Anguilla
Shoal Bay Scuba Fishing	(264) 235-1482	1.4 mi. North of Central Blowing Point

Fishing and chartering in Anguilla are not the easiest pastimes to pursue, but if you are passionate about fishing, it can be done, and is worth the work. Once you get out on the water, you'll be happy you did.

Golf

Golf on Anguilla is limited, but spectacular

Despite Anguilla's reputation of catering to upper class tourists, the availability of golf on the island is minimal. What the golf scene lacks in quantity, however, it makes up for in quality, so golf fanatics who can't bear to go their entire Anguillan vacation without teeing off can make arrangements to do so at one of the best courses in the Caribbean.

Anguilla Golf Association

The Anguilla Golf Association was formed in 2001, before a golf course even existed on the island. Through the help of the organization, two courses have since opened, and multiple golf education programs have come to fruition. Unfortunately, frequent visitors to Anguilla may not join the association, as one must be a local resident, property owner, or hold a valid work permit.

Anguilla's Golf Course

Once known as Tenemos Golf Club, Cuisinart Golf Club in West End is Anguilla's first (and only) full 18-hole championship golf course.

Named one of the Best Courses in the Caribbean and Mexico, the course is managed by the CuisinArt Resort & Spa. It was designed by Greg Norman and first built in 2006, then improved upon in 2011 when Cuisinart Resort took ownership. Picturesque views of Anguilla scenery are the focus of this moderately challenging course and recent renovations include a revamp of one of Anguilla's landmarks, Merrywing Salt Pond. Off in the distance, the island of Sint Maartencan be spotted from the course as well, particularly from the tee box at the first hole. The course is a total of 7,063 yards, and welcomes golfers of every skill level to try it out. Regular green fees begin at $180(USD), and you can rent clubs for $55(USD). You can contact the Cuisinart Golf Club at 264-498-5602.

Golf Courses

Name	Phone	Location	Island
CuisinArt Resort Golf Course	(264) 498-5602	CuisinArt Resort & Spa - Rendezvous Bay	Anguilla

Golf Events

Each year, golf brings its own set of tourists to the island of Anguilla. Many come simply to get a chance to play the CuisinArt golf course, while others come to participate in golf tournaments. The Ruben Brown Celebrity Golf Tournament is one that brings celebrities together in April to raise funds for a community project, such as a center for local youths. It is played by celebrities from the Caribbean and the U.S. that may not have pro-status golf skills, but are well-versed enough to make viewing interesting.

The latest golf event to arrive on Anguilla is the Anguilla Open Golf Tournament. The first was held in June of 2012 at the CuisinArt Resort & Spa. Over 100 talented golfers from the United States, Anguilla, Sint Maarten, Antigua, St. Kitts, St. Lucia, the Bahamas, Puerto Rico, and Guadeloupe paid a $300(USD) entry fee to participate in this championship event that could earn them several thousand dollars. The event was kicked off with an opening reception, and winners were recognized at the closing reception.

Golf in Anguilla is a possibility. Make sure to schedule your tee times in advance to ensure availability, and your dream of golfing with the Caribbean Sea as your backdrop is on its way to coming true.

Nightlife

There is more to do in Anguilla after the sun sets than one might expect

Despite being one of the smaller of the Caribbean islands, Anguilla still boasts a lively nightlife.

Often, visitors can spend their nights checking out the theatrical and musical reviews hosted by various resorts on the island, and most have bars on property as well. Still, if you'd like to get out and explore all of the after dark entertainment that the island has to offer, you will find there to be a variety of bars and even a few nightclubs to choose from. Check out Sandy Ground and Shoal Bay for the island's most popular haunts.

Bars

Housed in a boat, the Elvis Beach Bar is open Wednesday through Monday, and features live music every day it is open but Monday. The bar is known for its great rum punch and bar food.

Johnno's Beach Stop is a fun place to stop in for a drink. There is live music and dancing every night on the open air deck, and its location in Sandy Ground is prime for an eclectic bunch of patrons.

If you're looking for a place that is more restaurant than bar, hit up Palm Grove Bar and Grill. Seafood is on the menu here, and the johnnycakes are so good that the recipe has been published in *Bon Appétit*.

A few other bars in Anguilla include Ripples in South Hill; Rafes in Sandy Ground; and Elodias Beach, Hardbroke, Le Beach, Madeariman, and Uncle Ernie's in Shoal Bay.

Nightclubs

In a building that is made of driftwood is Dune Preserve, a music club at which reggae star Bankie Banks, and American actor Kevin Bacon regularly play. There is a beach bar, a dance floor, and a $15(USD) cover charge. Fodors recently ranked this spot as one of the "Top 16 Beach Bars in the World."

Converted from a rock-salt factory to a music club, is Pumphouse in Sandy Ground. Housed in the building is a mini museum of sorts featuring equipment from its factory days, but mainly patrons visit for the live music, dance floor, and drinks.

If you're one who loves to dance the night away in a crowd thick with other dancers, head over to the Red Dragon. A DJ spins dance music over the loud speakers, and the place is particularly packed on weekends.

Some of your best memories of Anguilla will be when you really let loose and allow yourself to relax. Whether you're dancing the night away, or simply hanging out bar side, Anguilla's nightlife will encourage you to let go.

Entertainment And Nightlife		
Name	Phone	Location
Bamboo Beer Box	--	Meads Bay
Beach Bar at CuisinArt	(264) 498-2000	Rendezvous Bay
Blanchards Beach Shack	https://www.facebook.com/BlanchardsBeachShack/	Meads Bay

Bar		
Blue Bar	(264) 462-1000	1.0 mi. West-Northwest of the Valley
Corner Bar and Pizza	(264) 497-3937	North Hill Village
D'Sand Pit	(264) 497-6827	West End
da'Vida Bar	--	Crocus Hill
Dad's Bar	(264) 581-3237	Sandy Ground Village
Dune Preserve Bar	(264) 497-6219	Rendezvous Bay
Elvis Beach Bar	(264) 772-0637	Sandy Ground Village
Falcon's Nest Bar	(264) 772-1127	Island Harbour
Garvey's Sunshine Shack	--	Rendezvous Bay
Gwen's Beach Bar	(264) 497-2120	Upper Shoal Bay
KazBar	(264) 498-2000	Rendezvous Bay
Maundays Club	--	Maundays Bay

Nat's Bar	(264) 497-4224	Junks Hole
Oasis Beach Bar	--	Shoal Bay West
Red Dragon Disco	(264) 497-2687	South Hill
Ripples Bar	--	Sandy Ground Village
Roy's Bayside Bar	--	Sandy Ground Village
Sandbar	--	Sandy Ground Village
Serenity Beach Bar	(264) 497-3328	Upper Shoal Bay
Smokey's Bar	--	Cove Bay
Sunset Bar	(877) 733-3611	Long Bay Village
Uncle Ernie's	(264) 497-3907	Shoal Bay East

Shopping

Shopping in Anguilla
If you are looking for a bargain, Anguilla may not be your first choice
Gifts and Souvenirs

If you're looking for some gifts or souvenirs you might want to try Beach Happy, which is located in Maundays Bay, in western Anguilla. Beach Happy offers you a wide range of women's and men's swimwear in both kid and adult sizes, as well as colorful cover-ups and t-shirts covered in the brand's catch-phrase, Don't Worry, Beach Happy. For when the sun is too hot or the waves are a little rough, Beach Happy offers you some great rash guards that you can wear over your swimsuit. For customers who want to call in advance, do so at (264) 582-4545.

Many gift and souvenir shops located in Anguilla are shown here:

GIFTS AND SOUVENIRS ON ANGUILLA

Name	Phone	Location
Anguilla National Trust Gift Shop	(264) 497-5054	The Valley, Central Anguilla
Anguilla Sea Salt Company	(264) 498-7258	1.7 mi. North-Northwest of Central East End
Beach Happy	(264) 582-4545	1.3 mi. South West of Central Meads Bay
Cards Plus	(264) 497-0225	Anguilla
Caribbean Silk Screen	(264) 497-2272	1.0 mi. North of Central Blowing Point
Le Petit Giftshop	(264) 497-	The Valley, Central Anguilla

	3730	
Sea Spray Gifts and Smoothies	(264) 497-7293	North Hill Village, Central Anguilla
Straw Hat Restaurant Shop	(264) 497-8300	0.1 mi. West-Southwest of Central Meads Bay

Specialty Shops

One of the more popular speciality shops in the area is Savannah Gallery. This store is found in central Anguilla. Since 1996, Savannah Gallery has been showcasing original Anguillan artwork from the confines of two historic homes located next to one another in the lower Historic Valley. They're on Coronation Avenue.

Another good option is Devonish Art Gallery, which is found 6.5 mi. (10.5 km) from Savannah Gallery. Courtney and Carrole Devonish are the proprietors of the Devonish Gallery, where they display and sell not only their own sculptures and ceramics, but also offer a space for local artisans to get their art out into the world. If you'd like to call before you go, do so at (264) 497-2949.

Bartlett's Collection: Handmade souvenirs from around the world are on display and available for purchase at Bartlett's Collection. The Barlett family shop began in the Netherlands, then made its way to Anguilla, where they now sell such items as beachwear, books,

Christmas ornaments, original paintings, and more. If you are looking to call in advance, you can do so at (264) 497-6625.

Many of the specialty shops located in Anguilla are provided down below.

Specialty Shops On Anguilla

Name	Type	Phone	Location
ALAK Art Gallery	Art Gallery	(264) 497-7270	2.4 mi. Northeast of Central the Valley
Anguilla Arts and Crafts Shop	Art Gallery	(264) 497-2200	Stoney Ground, Central Anguilla
Art Cafe	Art Gallery	(264) 497-8595	1.7 mi. North of Central East End
Bartlett's Collection	Art Gallery	(264) 497-6625	Sandy Ground Village, Central Anguilla
Cheddie's Carving Studio	Art Gallery	(264) 497-6027	1.0 mi. Northeast of Central Meads Bay
Devonish Art Gallery	Art Gallery	(264) 497-2949	0.9 mi. South West of Central Meads Bay
Diamonds International	Jewelry Store	--	Central Anguilla
Elegante Jewellery Shop	Jewelry Store	(264) 497-2074	Stoney Ground, Central Anguilla
L Bernbaum Art	Art Gallery	(264)	Sandy Ground Village

Gallery		497-5211	
Loblolly Gallery	Art Gallery	497-6006	Crocus Hill, Central Anguilla
Pineapple Gallery	Art Gallery	(264) 497-3609	Sandy Ground Village, Central Anguilla
Savannah Gallery	Art Gallery	(264) 497-2263	Central Anguilla
Tackle Box Sports Centre	Fishing Equipment and Tackle Shop	(264) 497-2896	Stoney Ground, Central Anguilla
World Fabrics	Fabric, Sewing and Needlework Supplies Store	(264) 497-3154	1.2 mi. North-Northwest of Central Blowing Point

Clothing and Apparel

Enjoy shopping for clothing? You might enjoy a visit to ZaZaa Boutique & Petitie ZaZaa -- which is located in Shoal Bay West, in western Anguilla. The motto at ZaZaa Boutique & Petitie ZaZaa is "Make it Anguillan!" Which means, when you walk into the shop, almost everything available to purchase was made by local hands Browse the wares here and perhaps you'll find the perfect souvenir for someone waiting back home. They are situated on West End Road .

A second option is Limin Boutique -- which is located approximately two miles (approximately three kilometers) to the northeast of ZaZaa Boutique & Petitie ZaZaa. Owners Ken and Renee choose each piece of merchandise that they sell. They typically go for well-made beach wear and jewelry, as well as souvenirs. You will be able to find them on Main Road.

A third apparel shop you might enjoy is Irie Life. Quality t-shirts for all members of the family in island prints and bright colors, back packs, purses, jewelry, art, collectable, and more made by real Caribbean artists are all available at this vivacious little shop. For customers who want to call ahead, do so at (264) 497-6526.

Many apparel shops in Anguilla can be seen here:

Clothing And Apparel On Anguilla

Name	Type	Phone	Location
A & S Sports Wear	General Clothing Store	(264) 497-8803	Stoney Ground, Central Anguilla
Ashani's Shoe Box	Shoe Store	(264) 497-0864	Stoney Ground, Central Anguilla
Azemmour	Boutique	(264) 497-6666	1.2 mi. South-Southwest of Central Meads Bay
Azemmour Boutique	Boutique	(264) 497-8852	1.3 mi. South-Southwest of Central Meads Bay
Beach'N Stuff	Swimwear, Beachwear and Sportswear Store	(264) 498-3224	Stoney Ground, Central Anguilla
Cap J	Boutique	(264) 497-6666	1.2 mi. South-Southwest of Central Meads Bay

Fashion Closet	Clothing Store	(264) 497-8252	Stoney Ground, Central Anguilla
Imanisha's Intimate Apparel & Body Shop	Lingerie Store	(264) 498-2110	Stoney Ground, Central Anguilla
Irie Life	General Clothing Store	(264) 497-6526	0.9 mi. North of Central Blowing Point
Janvel's Boutique	Boutique	(264) 497-2221	Blowing Point, Southwestern part of Anguilla
Jus Bangin Boutique	Boutique	(264) 497-2804	1.4 mi. East of Central Blowing Point
Kimmey's Fashion Boutique	General Clothing Store	(264) 497-3876	Stoney Ground, Central Anguilla
Limin Boutique	Boutique	(264) 53-3733	0.5 mi. East of Central Meads Bay
Petal's Boutique	Boutique	(264) 497-6442	0.1 mi. South West of Central Meads Bay
Safety Step	Clothing Store	(264) 497-4663	George Hill, Central Anguilla
Shop 4 Less Department Store Supermarket	Department Store	(264) 498-6060	North Hill Village, Central Anguilla
ZaZaa Boutique & Petitie ZaZaa	Boutique	(264) 497-6049	1.6 mi. South West of Central Meads Bay

Food and Grocery

Need to pick up some food supplies? Ashley & Sons Blowing Point is located within Blowing Point, in southwestern Anguilla. Your typical small, family-owned grocery, everything you need to keep the kitchen stocked is available here. The property is located on Blowing Point Road.

A second possibility is Le Petit Patissier, which is found 3.9 mi. (6.3 km) away from Ashley & Sons Blowing Point. Located on the property of Koal Keel, Le Petit Patissier is considered to be one of the top bakeries on Anguilla. Not only does this spot serve up a decadent selection of delicious baked goods, but the environment is beyond elegant, making you feel like sipping your tea with your pinky up and your napkin in your lap. If you would like to call before making reservations, do so at (264) 497-2930.

Mary's Bakery: Closed on Saturdays, Mary's opens early in the morning every other day of the week. They close at 8:00 p.m. To reach them, call (264) 497-2318.

View the chart below for more information about your options.

Food And Grocery Stores On Anguilla			
Name	Type	Phone	Location
Albert Marketplace	Grocery Store	(264) 497-2240	The Quarter, Central Anguilla

Alberta Lake Market	Grocery Store	--	The Valley, Central Anguilla
Anguilla Liquors & Tobacco Ltd.	Beer, Wine, and Liquor Store	(264) 497-2974	Stoney Ground, Central Anguilla
Ashley & Sons Blowing Point	Grocery Store	(264) 497-2641	0.3 mi. South of Central Blowing Point
Ashley's & Son's the Valley	Grocery Store	(264) 497-2641	The Valley, Central Anguilla
Best Buy Supermarket	Grocery Store	(264) 497-4444	1.5 mi. South West of Central East End
Food Ninety-Five	Grocery Store	(264) 497-6196	1.0 mi. South West of Central Meads Bay
Hungry's Fish Depot	Fish and Seafood Market	(264) 498-5041	Stoney Ground, Central Anguilla
Le Petit Patissier	Bakery	(264) 497-2930	The Valley, Central Anguilla
Les Grandes Vins De France	Beer, Wine, and Liquor Store	--	1.1 mi. Northwest of Central Blowing Point
Mary's Bakery	Bakery	(264) 497-2318	Stoney Ground, Central Anguilla
Merchant's Market	Grocery Store	(264) 497-5533	The Valley, Central Anguilla
Proctor's Market	Grocery Store	(264) 497-2445	The Valley, Central Anguilla
Sugar & Spice Bakery	Bakery	(264) 497-0099	George Hill, Central Anguilla

The Fishery	Fish and Seafood Market	(264) 497-3170	Stoney Ground, Central Anguilla

Snorkeling

Snorkeling Around Anguilla

As beautiful as the beaches of Anguilla are, would you believe that what lies beneath the surface of the sea may just be even more amazing? Just a few feet from the shore is a wondrous world filled with coral reefs, sunken ship wrecks, and curious fish all waiting for you to discover.

Snorkeling is a popular activity because anyone who is able to swim has the opportunity to enjoy the calming, yet still exciting activity. Donning a dive mask, swim fins, and a snorkel, snorkelers can remain under water for hours and explore Anguilla's shallow reefs. No training is required, and you can typically obtain snorkeling gear free of charge from your hotel or resort. If this is not a possibility, local dive shops offer equipment for purchase or for rent, and of course, you can always bring your own.

The great thing about the underwater world of Anguilla is that coral reefs surround the island, the waters tend to be calm, and visibility is excellent. This means almost every stretch of beach you encounter can be considered for snorkeling.

As snorkeling has proven to be so popular among tourists over the years, a few locals enlisted the help of the government to enlarge the natural reef through artificial measures such as sinking ships in strategic locations. In turn, they have created nurseries for fish who are able to thrive because of them. Thanks to these efforts, a series of five marine parks were created: Shoal Bay Reef, Little Bay, Sandy Island, Prickly Pear, and Dog Island; and now there are nearly twenty sanctioned dive sites, including four shipwrecks, that are also accessible by snorkelers.

If you're wondering exactly what type of fish you can expect to encounter, here are a few that are known to make an appearance: parrotfish, blue tags, snapper, baraccuda, angelfish, goat fish, eel, and even sea turtles on occasion.

Snorkeling Sites

If you're looking forward to experiencing what's below the surface you should consider a visit to Prickly Pear. One of the prime snorkeling spots around Anguilla, this area features some very clear water and nearly empty shores that make it a favorite place for marine life, as well as snorkelers. This snorkeling site is found within Prickely Pear Cays, in the western part of Anguilla.

Sandy Hill is another place you might enjoy. Home to a large reef, this is one of the best spots in Anguilla to catch a glimpse of some underwater action, as stingrays and fish are frequently found in the area. Additionally, since the beach is hardly ever crowded, snorkelers will rarely have to worry about there being too many swimmers in the water.

A third location to consider is Anguilla's Shoal Bay. With two reefs located just offshore, this is a great place to explore, no matter what your skill level. The larger of the two will take about forty-five minutes to complete, while the two together can take around an hour. Along the way you will see plenty of tropical fish and colorful coral.

A fourth place to go snorkeling is Little Bay. These protected waters offer great sights for snorkelers. Be on the look out for small fish, young sea turtles, and stingrays, all of which frequent the area. If you want to check it out, you'll find this site found within the central part of Anguilla.

Barnes Bay is a fifth location to consider. Just offshore lies a long reef that is filled with aquatic animals. Sea turtles, tropical fish, stingrays, and even squid can be found swimming about the area. Experienced snorkelers and confident swimmers can even go further out where the bigger fish reside.

Details concerning 13 of the best locations where you can go snorkeling in this area are listed here:

Snorkeling Sites Near Anguilla

Site	Location
Sandy Island Beach	2.9 mi. Northwest of Central Blowing Point
Prickly Pear	6.2 mi. North-Northwest of Central Meads Bay
Sandy Hill	1.0 mi. South West of Central East End
Anguilla's Shoal Bay	3.3 mi. North-Northeast of Central the Valley
Little Bay	Central Anguilla
Barnes Bay	0.9 mi. West-Southwest of Central Meads Bay
Crocus Bay	Central Anguilla
Meads Bay	0.2 mi. South West of Central Meads Bay
Scilly Cay Beach	1.8 mi. North of Central East End
Seafeathers Bay	0.7 mi. South of Central East End
Mimi Bay	0.7 mi. Southeast of Central East End
Pelican Bay	0.8 mi. East-Southeast of Central Blowing Point
Junks Hole	1.4 mi. Northeast of Central East End

Snorkeling Boat Trips

For some people, the most enjoyable snorkeling is accessed away from the shore.

If you're ready to combine some snorkeling with a boating adventure, you might want to check with Junior's Glass Bottom Boat. A whole new experience awaits you as you sail through the waters of Anguilla on a glass bottom boat that has a canopy and a cooler filled with soft drinks.

Another option worth investigating is Sail Chocolat. "The Best Way to See Anguilla" is by boat. This 35 foot Edel Catamaran offers guests the opportunity to do that in style as you explore some of the small islets that surround Anguilla. They're located in the Valley, in central Anguilla.

A third good option is Sea Pro Charters. Offering safe, comfortable, and reliable service for private boat charters, watersports tours, and an all around good times, these local captains have over 20 years of experience and really know their way around the waters between Anguilla, St. Martin, and St. Barths.

Information concerning boat trips and day sails that provide snorkeling opportunities are provided here:

Day Sails And Boat Trips On Anguilla

Name	Phone	Location
Calypso Charters	(246) 584-8504	0.4 mi. South of Central Blowing Point
Junior's Glass Bottom Boat	(264) 235-1008	2.9 mi. North-Northeast of Central the Valley
Sail Chocolat	(264) 497-3394	The Valley, Central Anguilla

Sea Pro Charters	(264) 584-0074	Sandy Ground Village, Central Anguilla

Snorkeling Services

If you're looking for someone that offers snorkel rentals, excursions, or similar services, you might want to check with Andy's Beach Rentals. While they actually specializes in rental car, Andy and his team is happy to help his guests explore all the best that Anguilla has to offer -- including what lies beneath the surface of the sea. Snorkeling is amazing in this area of the island, so pick up your snorkeling kit here before you drive off. They are situated in the southwestern part of Anguilla.

Another company worth knowing about is Calypso Charter's Snorkeling. Four hours of snorkeling will take you to destinations such as Dog Island, Prickly Pear, Sandy Island, Little Bay or Scilly Cay. Snorkeling equipment is available upon request as well as cold beverages.

A third option is Nature Boy Charters Snorkeling. Enjoy a day at the beach where you can also snorkel over picturesque coral reefs and view the tropical fish who live there. Snorkeling trips typically go to Little Bay, which is a protected marine park. They're located in the northern part of Anguilla.

The following chart enables you to get some key facts with regard to 4 companies that offer snorkeling services.

SNORKELING SERVICES ON ANGUILLA			
Name	Type	Phone	Location
Andy's Beach Rentals	Snorkeling Equipment Rental Service	(264) 584-7010	0.4 mi. South of Central Blowing Point
Calypso Charter's Snorkeling	Snorkeling Tour Operator	(264) 584-8504	0.4 mi. South of Central Blowing Point
Nature Boy Charters Snorkeling	Snorkeling Tour Operator	(264) 729-5587	Northern part of Anguilla
Shoal Bay Scuba Snorkeling	Snorkeling Tour Operator	(264) 235-1482	Sandy Ground Village, Central Anguilla

For more information about snorkeling, including tips and suggestions for both "old pros" and beginners, check out this comprehensive discussion of snorkeling in the Caribbean Book.

No matter where you stay on the island of Anguilla, you are just moments away from some of the best snorkeling in the region. Rent equipment or bring your own, just make sure you make time to get out and see what mysteries the sea has in store for you.

Spas in Anguilla

There are a number of ways to find peace and relaxation on Anguilla, from yoga retreats to wellness centers, but the island is increasingly becoming known as a great spa destination. Several resorts on the island have full service spas, and there are also a few independently operated facilities. Wherever you choose to stay on the island, you won't have to travel far to treat your body to the treatment it deserves -- and you'll soon have even more options, since several hotels have announced plans to add spas in the near future.

It shouldn't be hard to find a spa you like, considering that there are 10 spas located in this area.

If you're ready to indulge yourself, you can check with Spa at Viceroy Anguilla. An ocean side spa focused on rejuvenating to guests at the resort through numerous massage and beauty treatments. They are found in West End, in western Anguilla.

Another good option is Venus Spa. Venus has a long list of massage offerings including the Anguillan Massage, a Warmed Seashell Massage and the Caribbean Warm Stone Massage. Additional services, such as facials, waxings and other beauty treatments, are also available upon reservation. You can reach them at (264) 498-2000.

A third option is Auberge Spa. Achieve complete relaxation and peace at the Auberg Spa, where the professional therapists are ready and waiting to take care of you; mind, body and soul. They're situated in Long Bay Village, in western Anguilla.

Take a minute to read this table if you want some quick facts.

Spas On Anguilla

Name	Phone	Location
Auberge Spa	(786) 261-0800	0.5 mi. North-Northeast of Central Meads Bay
Body & Soul	(264) 235-8399	Sandy Ground Village, Central Anguilla
Cap Juluca Spa	(888) 858-5822 ext. 5514	1.2 mi. South-Southwest of Central Meads Bay
Malakh Day Spa	(264) 497-7251	2.9 mi. North-Northeast of Central the Valley
Spa at Viceroy Anguilla	(264) 497-7000	0.6 mi. West-Southwest of Central Meads Bay
The BlueSpa	(242) 462-1000	Central Anguilla
The Sri Balinese Petite Spa	(877) 647-4736	0.4 mi. South West of Central Meads Bay
Total Serenity Day Spa	(264) 476-6902	Anguilla
Venus Spa	(264) 498-2000	1.5 mi. West of Central Blowing Point
Zemi Thai House	(264) 584-0001	2.8 mi. North-Northeast of Central the Valley

Attractions

There are plenty of attractions for Anguilla's visitors to explore

Beach-going is the main draw for many of Anguilla's visitors -- in fact, many consider Anguilla's beaches to be among the most beautiful in the world. Its dazzling white sands and turquoise seas attract visitors to this tiny island paradise, but other interesting attractions add to Anguilla's interest.

Beaches

There are over 30 beaches in Anguilla, all of which are open to the public. Though many would agree that there is no such thing as a "bad" beach in Anguilla, if you want to know how to spot one of the best beaches, be on the lookout for a string of high-end resorts right along the shore line. The presence of these resorts will be a good indication that the beach front property is some of the most sought after on the island. Animal-lovers may be lucky enough to see turtles laying their eggs on the beach, but if not, crabs and lizards also abound. A few beaches also display striking stone formations, built by the waves as large pieces of coral wash ashore.

There are an abundance of beaches to enjoy on the island. Regardless of whether you prefer being around other people, or you prefer having more of the sand to yourself, you can find what you want. Just click on each beach name for a detailed article concerning that section of the coast.

Sandy Ground Beach: Sandy Ground Beach is one of the most popular beaches in all of Anguilla. This strip of sand is busy day and night with its many piers and just as numerous bars and nightlife options.

Another alternative to consider is Junks Hole. Junk's Hole is easily accessible by road. It's fairly isolated once you're there, but there is a nearby bar.

Sandy Island Beach: Barbecues, cabanas, cold drinks and the sun are what defines Sandy Island Beach. While the island was once known only to a few lucky travelers, the addition of some low impact tourist development has made this into a must do for guests who can make their way here.

Anguilla has several other beaches to choose from. Read from Anguilla Beach page for more information if you want to learn some more facts.

Although much of Anguilla is only lightly developed, you can still get a sense of its history. Several small museums and a few private collectors welcome visitors to view their artifacts. Anguilla's past is full of intriguing stories. There is only one surviving plantation house that shows what life was like in the 18th and 19th centuries. But other historic buildings have also been restored, with some of them now home to small businesses, including a famous restaurant. At the Old Salt Factory and Pump House, tours demonstrate the inner workings of this once-important island industry.

Museums

Assuming you enjoy learning about other people and places, you should consider visiting a museum during your time on Anguilla.

One popular destination is Wallblake House. It is located within the Valley, in central Anguilla. Tour hours are Tuesday and Friday, 10:00 am - Noon.

Many travelers also choose to visit Heritage Museum Collection. It is Island Harbour, in northeastern Anguilla. The museum is open from Monday through Friday from 10:00 a.m. to 5:00 p.m.

The table below has more details concerning some the available museums on the island.

Museums On Anguilla		
Name	Phone	Location
Heritage Museum Collection	(264) 235-7440	1.1 mi. North of Central East End
Wallblake House	(264) 497-6613	The Valley, Central Anguilla

Historical Sites

If you like to experience the history of foreign countries, you might enjoy visiting a few of these historical sites during your vacation.

A landmark that often intrigues visitors is Old Factory. It is located in the Valley, in central Anguilla. While most of the original ginning machinery was lost after the Old Factory was closed, what remains has been put on display for guests visiting the Tourist Office to peruse.

Another popular destination is Warden's Place. It is found in central Anguilla. Just like many of the Caribbean Islands, Anguilla depended, in part, on the sugar trade. Warden's Place was once a sugar plantation that was built in the 1790's.

Old Fort at Sandy Hill: Overlooking Sandy Hill Bay, this old fort was the colonist and British took their final stand against an invading French Force in 1796. In the end, the French were defeated and thanks to "The Battle of Anguilla", the island remained part of the British Empire.

Take a minute to read this table for a listing of historical sites on the island.

Historic Sites On Anguilla

Name	Phone	Location
Old Factory	(264) 497-2759	The Valley, Central Anguilla

Old Fort at Sandy Hill	--	1.8 mi. South West of Central East End
Old Salt Factory and Pump House	(264) 497-2711	Sandy Ground Village, Central Anguilla
Warden's Place	(264) 497-2930	Central Anguilla

Miscellaneous Landmarks

Vacationers will experience some other worthwhile places worth visiting on Anguilla.

The other types of landmarks on Anguilla are displayed below.

Miscellaneous Landmarks On Anguilla		
Name	Type	Location
Dolphin Discovery	Attraction	0.5 mi. South of Central Blowing Point
The Anguilla Aqua Park	Attraction	0.9 mi. Southeast of Central Meads Bay

Caves

Although most people visiting the area have heard about the beaches, those aren't the only way to experience the natural beauty of the land. Anguilla offers multiple choices, including a couple of caves.

The table right below lists a few details regarding caves.

CAVES ON ANGUILLA		
Name	Type	Location
Dropsey Bay Cave	Cave	1.9 mi. South West of Central East End
Goat Cave	Cave	2.9 mi. Northeast of Central East End

Parks

Travelers can visit the local park on Anguilla.

PARKS ON ANGUILLA			
Name	Type	Location	Island
Coronation Park	Park	The Valley, Central Anguilla	Anguilla

Land Formations

Another fun idea is to visit some of the more interesting area land formations. Other options like these on Anguilla are shown in the table below.

Land Formations On Anguilla		
Name	Type	Location
Barnes Bay	Bay	0.9 mi. West-Southwest of Central Meads Bay
Benzie's Bay	Bay	Central Anguilla
Black Garden Bay	Bay	2.1 mi. North-Northwest of Central the Valley

Bucks Bay	Bay	1.6 mi. Northwest of Central Blowing Point
Cove Pond	Pond	0.8 mi. South of Central Meads Bay
Golf Pond	Pond	1.5 mi. South West of Central Meads Bay
Grey Pond	Pond	1.0 mi. Northeast of Central East End
Junk's Hole Bay	Bay	2.0 mi. Northeast of Central East End
Katouche Bay	Bay	Central Anguilla
Long Bay	Bay	1.0 mi. Northeast of Central Meads Bay
Long Pond	Pond	1.8 mi. South West of Central East End
Maundays Bay	Bay	1.4 mi. South-Southwest of Central Meads Bay
Meads Bay	Bay	0.3 mi. North-Northwest of Central Meads Bay
Meads Bay Pond	Pond	0.3 mi. East of Central Meads Bay
Pelican Bay	Bay	0.8 mi. East-Southeast of Central Blowing Point
Road Bay	Bay	Central Anguilla
Road Salt Pond	Pond	Sandy Ground Village, Central Anguilla
Seafeathers Bay	Bay	0.9 mi. South-Southeast of Central East End
Sherrick's Bay	Bay	0.4 mi. West-Southwest of Central Shoal Bay West
West End Pond	Pond	1.6 mi. South West of Central Meads Bay

Visitors seeking to escape the everyday in a world-class, stunning setting will be thrilled to discover Anguilla.

Beaches in Anguilla

For discriminating travelers, Anguilla's beaches are unsurpassed

Even in the Caribbean, where beaches rule, Anguilla's beaches are known for being the best of the best. Soft, brilliant-white sands stretch out against clear blue waters. While there are other things to do on the island, spending time in the sand and surf is the number-one reason to come here.

In spite of Anguilla's small size, it boasts more than 30 spectacular beaches. All beaches are open to the public, though some of them can only be accessed by walking through hotels. The most popular beaches can get crowded, but you'll find the majority to be havens of tranquility. Bars and restaurants skirt some of them, so beach-goers can stroll right from lounge chair to dining chair.

Some of the more popular beaches are mentioned on this page. Additional discussion can be found in our beach guide for both Blowing Point and the Valley.

The west side is where you'll find many of the island's best beaches, lined by the most expensive resorts. Still, you really can't go wrong anywhere on Anguilla. Whether you're looking for swimming, windsurfing, a quiet retreat, or a wild shore to explore, you can find a suitable beach on any part of the island.

With peaceful waves, many beaches are good for swimming. However, strong currents and dangerous undertows make a few areas too treacherous for a dip in the water. This is especially true near Anguilla's northernmost tip, though rough spots are scattered here and there around the island. But they're still excellent places for picnicking, hiking, or watching the boats go by.

Pick Your Ideal Beach

You will discover a large selection of beaches to enjoy on the island. Whether you prefer being around other people, or you prefer a more secluded spot, you can find a beach that fits your preferences. You can click on the name of each beach to get additional information about that particular stretch of sand.

A nice beach where you can go snorkeling is Sandy Island Beach. Barbecues, cabanas, cold drinks and the sun are what defines Sandy Island Beach. While the island was once known only to a few lucky travelers, the addition of some low impact tourist development has made this into a must do for guests who can make their way here.

Another good option for snorkelers is Scilly Cay Beach. Part of the Scilly Cay Restaurant property, Scilly Cay Beach is one of the most popular tourist attractions in Anguilla. Heading over to Scilly Cay will give you the experience of a luxurious private-island resort without the price (though buying lunch on the island is about $100 per couple).

Anguilla's Shoal Bay: Shoal Bay is one of the most popular beaches on Anguilla. Not that any beach here could be called crowded, but you're certain to catch at least a few other people enjoy the sugar sand and crystalline waters of Shoal Bay.

Check out this table to learn more.

Beaches On Anguilla

Name	Location	Coast
Anguilla's Shoal Bay	3.3 mi. North-Northeast of Central the Valley	North East
Barnes Bay	0.8 mi. West-Southwest of Central Meads Bay	South West
Blackgarden Bay Beach	1.8 mi. North-Northwest of Central the Valley	North
Blowing Point Beach	0.4 mi. South of Central Blowing Point	South
Captain's Bay	2.4 mi. Northeast of Central East End	East
Corito Bay Beach	1.6 mi. South of Central the Valley	South
Cove Bay	0.8 mi. South of Central Meads Bay	South West
Crocus Bay	Central Anguilla	South East
Dropsey Bay Beach	1.9 mi. South West of Central East End	--
Elsie Bay Beach	1.9 mi. South-Southwest of Central the Valley	South
Forest Bay North	Forest Bay, Central Anguilla	South East
Island Harbour	1.7 mi. North of Central East End	North East

Junks Hole	1.3 mi. Northeast of Central East End	East
Katouche Bay Beach	North Hill Village, Central Anguilla	North
Limestone Bay Beach	Central Anguilla	North
Little Bay	Central Anguilla	East
Little Harbour	1.2 mi. East of Central Blowing Point	South
Maundays Bay Beach	1.2 mi. South-Southwest of Central Meads Bay	South West
Meads Bay	0.2 mi. South West of Central Meads Bay	South West
Merrywing Bay Beach	1.1 mi. Southeast of Central Meads Bay	South West
Mimi Bay	0.7 mi. East-Southeast of Central East End	East
Rendezvous Bay	1.3 mi. West of Central Blowing Point	South West
Road Bay	1.4 mi. North of Central Blowing Point	South West
Sandy Ground Beach	Sandy Ground Village, Central Anguilla	North
Sandy Hill	1.0 mi. South West of Central East End	East
Sandy Island Beach	2.9 mi. Northwest of Central Blowing Point	West-Southwest
Sandy Point Beach	0.5 mi. South of Central Blowing Point	South West
Scilly Cay Beach	1.9 mi. North of Central East End	North East
Sherricks Bay Beach	0.4 mi. West of Central Shoal Bay West	South West
Shoal Bay West	2.0 mi. South West of Central Meads Bay	South West
Sile Bay Beach	1.0 mi. East-Northeast of Central East End	South East

If you are looking for a wider selection of attractions beyond the category on this page, you should think about other locations. Read from our Attraction page concerning other interesting attractions for Anguilla.

For a fun diversion, some beaches offer water sports. Large hotels often provide equipment to their guests, so if you're staying at one you may be able to get all you need and head right out to the water. Parasailing, water-skiing, paddle-boating, and more await you. Coral reefs teeming with marine life make for magnificent snorkeling and scuba diving. Several old shipwrecks also can be investigated by certified divers. If you're not quite that adventurous, you can still see underwater wonders on a glass bottom boat tour.

Casinos

Casino lovers can enjoy a short ferry ride to nearby gambling

Many vacationers enjoy gambling as a method of letting go of their inhibitions and excite at the chance to roll the dice. Unfortunately, due largely to the highly religious nature of the island inhabitants, travelers will find no casinos on the island of Anguilla.

An effort was made during the 1980s to establish the development of a casino on Anguilla, but a deeply conflicted debate surrounding the issue prevented it from ever being built. The island's Church Council actively ensures that the ban on casinos is continually enforced, but travelers hankering for a night of gambling can satisfy their urge on the nearby island of St. Maarten.

With just a short ferry ride and a quick trip in a taxi cab, vacationers can travel to and from Anguilla to St. Maarten's bustling casino area. With 14 different casinos to choose from, travelers are sure to be pleased by the selection of gambling facilities. Guests can choose from casinos located within hotels, like the Princess Casinoand the Westin Casino, or gambling establishments that stand on their own property, such as the Jump-Up Casino. One of the best options for Anguilla vacationers visiting St. Maarten to gamble is the Princess Casino. If you're a high roller, head to the Casino Royale. This casino boasts the highest table limits anywhere on the island. Gamblers will discover that the casinos in St. Maarten offer a wide selection of games. If you're interested in bingo, head down to the Rouge Et Noir Casino. Nearly every casino on the island features blackjack, roulette and multiple versions of poker, as well as slot machines.

While Anguilla hosts no casinos on the island due to governmental restrictions, guests will find that seeking a night of gambling is only a short island hop away. If you want to have an entertaining evening without leaving Anguilla, consider exciting alternatives like dancing at the Red Dragon Disco or heading to a hotel for a beach barbecue complete with local calypso-style musical performances.

Landmarks

Anguilla's landmarks include a few historical buildings, and some architecture that will take your breath away

Anguilla is more than resort hotels and beautiful beaches. There is a culture and a history on the island that tourists would be sorry if they missed out on. Learning about the island is as simple as visiting a few local landmarks.

Places of Worship

It is not the historical significance, or stories of martyrs that draws visitors to the churches of Anguilla. Instead, it is the architecture that attracts on-lookers. Many of the island's tourists don't seek out the churches, but once you notice one, you begin to take note of the others.

The Bethel Methodist Church in Sandy Ground is an excellent example of Anguillan stonework, and the stained glass windows are a work of art. In The Valley, the three arches on the front of St. Gerard's Catholic Church, and the colorful collection of stonework that covers them are simply breathtaking.

Sombrero Lighthouse

Anguilla's Sombrero Island is home to the Sombrero Lighthouse. The lighthouse was built originally in 1868, but had to be rebuilt in 1962 after it was destroyed during Hurricane Donna. Sombrero Lighthouse is something of a national treasure, having consistently appeared on Anguilla stamps since the 1950s.

Museums

In case you like to explore other people and places, you should consider visiting a museum during your vacation. Click on each name to read full details.

A landmark worth visiting is Wallblake House. It is located in the Valley, in central Anguilla. Tour hours are Tuesday and Friday, 10:00 am - Noon.

Another common landmark for vacationers is Heritage Collection Museum. It is Island Harbour, in northeastern Anguilla. The museum is open from Monday through Friday from 10:00 a.m. to 5:00 p.m.

The following table provides you with some details concerning a few the museums you might enjoy on the island.

Museums On Anguilla

Name	Phone	Location
Heritage Collection Museum	(264) 235-7440	1.1 mi. North of Central East End
Wallblake House	(264) 497-6613	The Valley, Central Anguilla

Historical Sites

Enjoy learning some of the history of the places you visit? If that's the case, you should consider visiting one or two of these historical attractions during your vacation.

If you are looking to do some sight-seeing, visit Old Factory. It is located in the Valley, in central Anguilla. The Anguilla Tourist Office, and thus the Old Factory, is open from 10:00 a.m. to 4:00 p.m., closing from noon to 1:00 p.m.

Another interesting landmark worth visiting is Warden's Place. It is located in central Anguilla. Just like many of the Caribbean Islands, Anguilla depended, in part, on the sugar trade. Warden's Place was once a sugar plantation that was built in the 1790's.

Old Fort at Sandy Hill: Overlooking Sandy Hill Bay, this old fort was the colonist and British took their final stand against an invading French Force in 1796. In the end, the French were defeated and thanks to "The Battle of Anguilla", the island remained part of the British Empire.

Be sure to look through the following table for a list of historic sites on the island.

Historic Sites On Anguilla		
Name	Phone	Location
Old Factory	(264) 497-	The Valley, Central Anguilla

	2759	
Old Fort at Sandy Hill	--	1.8 mi. South West of Central East End
Old Salt Factory and Pump House	(264) 497-2711	Sandy Ground Village, Central Anguilla
Warden's Place	(264) 497-2930	Central Anguilla

Miscellaneous Landmarks

Vacationers can experience some other interesting attractions on the island.

The chart just below provides some details concerning other kinds of attractions of interest to travelers.

Miscellaneous Landmarks On Anguilla		
Name	Type	Location
Dolphin Discovery	Attraction	0.5 mi. South of Central Blowing Point
The Anguilla Aqua Park	Attraction	0.9 mi. Southeast of Central Meads Bay

If you are seeking a wider selection of points of interest beyond just these, you can look farther afield. For more in-depth coverage of other attractions, read from Attraction page in this book.

Natural Attractions

Anguilla's small size means that visitors can hike from one attraction to the next

Take a deep breath in. If the air isn't warm, fresh, and filled with the scent of white cedar, you probably aren't outdoors in Anguilla enjoying all the natural sites the island has to offer.

Tourists who yearn to get outside and explore have a number of hiking trails to venture out on, the possibility of saddling up and going on a horseback tour, and the once-in-a-lifetime opportunity of watching the nesting habits of a variety of sea turtles.

Caves

Anguilla has an interesting collection of caves that are known for their mysterious nature that tourists simply can't resist. Each cave is unique. Dropsey Bay Cave is a small cave with an underground bridge that is inviting to snorkelers, while Goat Cave is better for non-swimmers. Take a look below for the locations of these underground wonders.

Caves	
Name	Location
Dropsey Bay Cave	1.9 mi. (3.0 km) South West of East End
Goat Cave	6.5 mi. (10.5 km) Northeast of the Valley

Nature Tours And Guides		
Name	Type	Location

| Dolphin Discovery | Dolphin Encounter Service | 0.5 mi. (0.8 km) South of Blowing Point |
| Nature Explorers Anguilla | Nature Tourism Service | Northern part of The Valley |

Hiking

Because Anguilla is only 17 miles long at its greatest length, hiking to see the sites is a very real possibility. There are numerous locations along the coast line where projects to create new real estate began, but were never completed, and these paved paths make for excellent hiking locations.

In 2010, the Anguilla Archaeological and Historical Society, Anguilla Hotel and Tourism Association, Anguilla National Trust, and the Anguilla Tourist Board joined forces to create the Anguilla Heritage Trail. Though other sites will be added to the trail in the future, when the Anguilla Heritage Trail had it's grand opening, there were ten sites marked along the trail. These sites are all historical and important to the island's culture, and include Crocus Hill, the Factory, Heritage Collection, Katouche Bay, Old Valley Well, Pumphouse, Rendezvous Bay, Sandy Ground, Wallblake House, and Wardens Place. Along with these sites are 30 directional signs to guide hikers and drivers along the trail.

Other hiking trails throughout the island include the following:

Hiking Trails In Anguilla

Trail	Location	Sites
Crocus Hill to Limestone Bay	The Valley	Blackgarden Bay, Roaches Hill, Little Bay
Island Harbour through Brimegin	Near The Valley	Pitch Apple Hole, Shole Bay, goats
Katouche Valley	Katouche Valley	Forest lands, beach
Savannah Bay to Mimi Bay	Between Junks Hole and East End Village	Salt pond, Caribbean Sea rock formations
Windward Point	Island Harbour	Captains Bay, Abadam Hole, view of St. Barts, view of Scrub Island, view of Little Scrub, goats, lizard, birds

Always be sure to wear clothes that are light weight, but cover your body to protect you from bugs, and hiking boots to protect your feet. You'll also want to be sure to bring plenty of water along with you.

Horseback Riding

If equine exploration is your thing, Anguilla is a great choice in the Caribbean. There are a few stables and tours that allow tourists to traverse the island on horseback. **Seaside Stables**, for example, takes guests out on rides along the beach. Options include daylight and moonlight rides, and some guests are even permitted to swim on horseback. Tours within the interior of the island are also available. Prices range from $60 to $85(USD) an hour.

Animal Attractions

Between the months of April and November, visitors have the opportunity to view a rare, and wondrous site. It is during this time of year that the green, hawksbill, and leatherback sea turtles makes the **beaches of Anguilla** their nesting grounds. The Anguilla National Trust can direct you on the proper course of action to take to properly view the nesting grounds without interfering with the sea turtles natural process. Some of the best beaches to do this include Captains Bay and Meads Bay.

OTHER NATURAL ATTRACTIONS		
Name	Type	Location
Cove Pond	Pond	Cove Bay
Grey Pond	Pond	4.8 mi. (7.7 km) East-Northeast of the Valley
Long Pond	Pond	2.3 mi. (3.8 km) East of the Valley
Maundays Bay	Bay	Maundays Bay
Sherrick's Bay	Bay	4.7 mi. (7.5 km) West of Blowing Point
West End Pond	Pond	West End

The outside world of Anguilla offers visitors a variety of opportunity to get out and explore.

Cruising to Anguilla

Anguilla is a quiet and peaceful Caribbean cruise port of call

Without rampant duty-free shopping and other tourist attractions, Anguilla is not among the most popular destinations for cruise liners in the Caribbean. Still, there are several cruise lines that are drawn to Anguilla's peaceful seclusion, good food, and unparalleled beaches.

With neighboring St. Maarten attracting hordes of cruise travelers to its beaches and duty-free shopping, Anguilla remains a considerably quieter destination. Cruise travelers who do choose one of the few cruise lines that call on Blowing Point Harbor in Anguilla will be richly rewarded with resplendent beaches and world class French, Italian, and eclectic cuisine. Large cruise vessels carrying thousands of passengers do not come to this island. But smaller luxury lines allow their limited numbers of guests to enjoy a day snorkeling, scuba diving, or simply sunbathing at one of the island's 33 beaches. While the island is not know for shopping, there is a fine assortment of local crafts and goods to be purchased.

Cruise season in the Caribbean occurs during the tourist high season of mid-December to mid-April, when cooler temperatures north of the equator convince vacationers to head to more tropical climates. Hurricane season, which can pose problems and complications for Caribbean travelers, ends in November. Cruise fares during the off season can be lower than high season fares, although the limited number of cruise lines traveling to Anguilla may make it difficult to find cruises during any part of the year. A few of the lines have just a small number of cruises that will call on Anguilla.

Cruises can be ideal for travelers who do not wish to plan their vacation around one single island. Cruises depart from destinations in southern Florida and other Caribbean islands. Travelers who have chosen to stay on Anguilla for an extended vacation can charter a day cruise to one of the small offshore islands.

Major Cruise Lines

Cruise Line	Contact Information	Sample Itinerary
Compagnie des Iles de Ponant	http://www.ponant.com/	Point-a-Pitre, Antigua, Virgin Gorda, Jost van Dyke, Anguilla, St. Martin, St. Barthelemy, Point-a-Pitre
Crystal Cruises	2049 Century Park East Suite 1400 Los Angeles, CA 90067 866-446-6625 http://www.crystalcruises.com	Miami, Grand Turk, Anguilla, Tortola, St. Barthelemy, St. Thomas, Miami
	2601 South Bayshore Drive	St. Thomas, St. John, Virgin

SeaDream Yacht Club	Penthouse1B Coconut Grove, FL 33133 800-707-4911 305-631-6110 (Fax) http://www.seadreamyachtclub.com E-mail: info@seadreamyachtclub.com	Gorda, Jost van Dyke, Saba, St. Barthelemy, Anguilla, St. Martin
Star Clippers	7200 NW 19th Street, Suite 206 Miami, FL 33126 305-442-0550 800-442-0551 305-442-1611 (Fax) http://www.starclippers.com/ E-mail: info@starclippers.com	St. Maarten, Anguilla, Virgin Gorda, Norman Island, Jost van Dyke, St. Kitts, St. Barthelemy, St. Maarten
Windstar Cruises	300 Elliott Avenue West Seattle, WA 98119 206-281-3535 800-258-7245 206-286-3229 (Fax) http://www.windstarcruises.com E-mail: info@windstarcruises.com	St. Thomas, St. John, Anguilla, St. Martin, St. Barthelemy, Iles des Saintes, St. Lucia, Bequia, Virgin Gorda, St. Thomas

These companies tend to have smaller cruise vessels that focus on providing passengers with a luxury experience. Services and amenities on board these luxury liners will include watersports, bars, spa services, libraries, and numerous restaurants. The largest liner traveling to Anguilla will hold a little more than 1,000 passengers, while many others will hold 100 to 200 passengers. Travelers who have problems with motion sickness may experience more trouble on board smaller cruise vessels.

Luxury cruises aboard small ships will often give travelers a high level of customer care and service. Prospective cruisers should pay attention to the number of on board service staff members in comparison to the guest capacity. Typically, the lower the ratio of guests to staff, the higher the level of customer service. Also important in determining the size and dimension of the boat is the gross registered tonnage, which indicates the volume and size. Travelers can compare the dimensions and area of the boat to determine the ratio of space to passengers.

Some cruise lines may also offer themed cruises that target a certain type of traveler. These may be geared towards groups such as older couples, singles, or gays and lesbians. Some companies even allow their smaller vessels to be chartered by companies and individuals who would like to host events during a Caribbean cruise.

Class and Cabin

Although smaller cruise lines typically aim to provide luxury class cruise experiences, some will also provide value cruises. Some cruises may offer travelers the opportunity to select from a number of classes. Higher class fares give travelers more spacious and luxurious cabins.

The quality of meals, products, and waitstaff attention will also increase with the fare.

Cabins on cruise ships are generally divided into two categories: "run of the ship" and perfect. Passengers who select "run of the ship" cabins are able to request an outer or an inner cabin, but are not allowed to select a specific room. Travelers will be unsure of their room assignment until their cruise sets sail. Perfect cabins give travelers the ability to select a specific cabin of their choice. Perfect cabins have the additional benefit of allowing travelers to select rooms that are away from noisy or high traffic areas such as bars and gyms. Travelers with children should beware of outer cabins with open balconies.

Packing and Costs

Beach and active wear are important types of clothing to pack when visiting Anguilla and the Caribbean. Many travelers who disembark on the island will want to spend the day enjoying one of the magnificent white sand beaches. Travelers should also bring hats, sunglasses, and sunscreen in order to ward off the strong Caribbean sun. Travelers who plan on shopping or dining in Anguilla should remember that wearing beachwear and other types of revealing clothing is considered inappropriate away from the beach. Dinner generally requires pants and casual dresses. Travelers should ask about cruise line dress codes for events and dining rooms.

Shopping is not a popular tourist pastime on Anguilla, but travelers may want to set aside a budget to look for small crafts and local goods. Island tours, watersports, and other recreational activities can also drive up the overall cost of a cruise vacation. Select cruise lines may have all-inclusive packages that cover tips and activities, while others may require passengers to pay extra fees for these things. Plan a daily spending budget to cover these expenses.

Travelers who choose to cruise to Anguilla are likely to enjoy a warm welcome from the inviting beaches and friendly residents.

Planning Your

Planning Your Vacation in Anguilla
Travelers have much to consider as they plan a trip to Anguilla
With so much information to understand and explore, planning a trip to Anguillacan be exciting as well as slightly intimidating. This guide will put you at ease by explaining all of the necessary steps you must take when traveling to this gorgeous and untouched island.

Travelers should realize that Anguilla does not have the large scale shopping or other attractions that islands such as St. Maarten have. Anguilla is known for its fine food and lovely beaches, but travelers who desire lots of shops and entertainment may be dissapointed. Luckily, a day trip to St. Martin for the added tourist attractions can easily be arranged via ferry.

Meanwhile, if you are looking for a peaceful vacation with bountiful opportunities for dining, then Anguilla is your island. If you are still trying to decide whether to go to Anguilla or not, read on Why Not Go page in this book. If you have made the decision to visit, some careful planning will help you create your dream vacation.

Getting Info

Begin by learning more about life on the island. Learn about how locals interact, opportunities for eco-tourism, and whether you need to bring electrical converters or adapters. You can consult a number of resources on these subjects, including other articles on this site, as well as books and magazines.

When to Go

Trade winds cool the tropical temperatures in Anguilla, keeping the climate pleasant, even in the summer. The island is also fairly dry, meaning that vacations may not necessarily be rained out during the summer rainy season. However, hurricane season, which lasts from June to November, is an important consideration for all travelers. The most popular time to visit the island is the tourist season of mid-December to mid-April.

Making Decisions

Travelers can visit the island by taking a flight from neighboring islands such as St. Maarten or Puerto Rico, or by taking to the ocean aboard a small cruise vessel or yacht. Once on the island, travelers must choose where to stay and how to get around. Beaches are never far away, but accommodations and beaches are concentrated in the southwest and northeast areas of the county.

Travelers should plan on visiting a number of beaches during their stay, as they all have their own distinct qualities. Some visitors will want to make arrangements for scuba diving, snorkeling, or a day cruise. Shoppers can find a number of crafts and goods on the island or take the ferry to St. Maarten for entertainment and duty-free shopping.

Booking Your Trip

As prospective travelers weigh their vacation options, they will undoubtedly begin to think about their choices for booking their vacation. Although the Internet has become the most popular way of securing travel reservations, vacationers may also arrange for the services of a travel agent or phone representative.

After deciding to visit Anguilla, travelers can use their research to begin dreaming of the island's alluring beaches.

Booking

Booking your Trip to Anguilla
Travelers have several options when booking their island vacation

Now that you've made several important decisions including how you'll get to Anguilla, the kind of accommodations you want, and the activities that interest you, it's time to actually book your trip. Travelers have several options for making travel arrangements. Most people will want to find the best deals for their money, and these are often found on the Internet.

Online buying has grown in popularity over the past few years, and many people have taken advantage of the convenience of making travel arrangements via the Internet. You're also more likely to find the best traveling deals online. Travelers who are using this Web site to research an upcoming trip are among the vacationers who may feel comfortable booking a trip online. Always be careful when making your vacation arrangements over the Internet, even though using your credit card online is generally quite safe.

Vacationers will discover that there are many Internet-only deals that are not offered when calling the hotel or airline directly. Sometimes these companies may not even be aware of the online offers. By doing the research yourself, you can find the best deals and packages before you make any final decisions about your vacation.

Some people are more comfortable making their arrangements through a travel agent. Before you book your Anguilla trip over the phone, realize that with all the research you've already done online, you may know more about your vacation destination than your trusted travel agent, whose area of specialty may not even be the Caribbean. Why pay someone to do the investigating that you've already done? After all the time you've put into researching your vacation, you can make use of that information yourself.

Internet vendors offer a wide range of specialties. You can find vendors that sell travel all around the world and ones that specialize in a particular region. You may want to choose a vendor that specializes in Caribbean travel for your vacation to Anguilla. Often, vendors whose main market is the Caribbean will have a larger variety of accommodations available.

Online vendors usually have similar price ranges because they're in competition for your business. If you find a big price variation among several vendors, do a little more research to clear up any confusion. The major price differences can be accounted for by the companies' different ways of listing taxes and fees involved in making your purchases.

Making your reservations through a particular vendor will show your support for that company, so consider all of your options before picking one. Ask yourself a few questions, such as: was the vendor helpful, and was the information easy to find? After you've found an online vendor that you're comfortable with, booking your Anguilla vacation should be a breeze. Get ready for some fun in the sun on the lovely Caribbean island of Anguilla.

Budgeting

How Much Will it Cost to Vacation in Anguilla?

Travelers should consider the costs of their vacation as they plan their trip

Anguilla can be one of the most expensive destinations in the Caribbean, with luxurious resorts and world class restaurants catering to discriminating travelers and celebrities. Travelers on more modest funds can still enjoy a trip to Anguilla, as long as they realistically plan their budget.

Luckily, although traveling to and vacationing in Anguilla can be expensive; the luxury of enjoying the island's mesmerizing beauty comes free of charge. While travelers will certainly save money by spending a day lounging at the beach, there are a number of significant costs that should also be considered. Once travel arrangements have been made, the two primary costs for travelers will be accommodations and dining. Other daily spending needs may include the cost of transportation, tours, and eco-tourism activities. Shopping, taxes, and tips are additional expenses to consider. Although it can be frightening to discover how much you may spend on your vacation, carefully planning a budget should allow you to plan a trip that will meet your expectations without emptying your bank account.

Lodging

Although Anguilla does not particularly cater to travelers looking for large all-inclusive resort complexes, some of the finest resorts and hotels in the Caribbean are situated along the island's sparkling beaches. These resorts and hotels have restaurants, meal plans, water sports, bars, and other amenities for travelers to enjoy. Additionally, these resorts often offer vacation packages that highlight spa treatments, food and wine, or honeymoon activities.

Another popular option in Anguilla is to rent one of the island's many villas, condos, or apartments. These tend to be pricey, but are luxurious and spacious accommodations that can provide a temporary island home for travelers. Finally, there is an assortment of reasonably priced hotels and small inns to choose from on the island.

While the price of accommodations in Anguilla can be high, traveling during the Caribbean off-season may allow travelers to stay in some of the nicer resorts on the island. Prices and rates during the Caribbean off-season can be reduced by up to 50 percent, and the prices of vacation packages also drop considerably. On the other hand, many hotels and restaurants may close during the off season, particularly in September and October. Rates at hotels and resorts are often for double occupancy rooms, and additional guests can incur fees. Carefully inspect hotel policies, fees, and charges before committing. Hotel bills will have a 10 percent tax and a service charge that is typically between 10 and 15 percent.

Packages that resemble all-inclusive deals at hotels and resorts cost from $1,760(USD) to around $10,000(USD) for stays of varying lengths. Regular rates at hotels and resorts can start as low as $90(USD) in some of the smallest inns, and move up to $245(USD) to $1,000(USD) a night. The luxury suites and villas at hotels can run travelers from $3,000(USD) to $6,450(USD). Meal plans can cost around $60(USD) per day, per guest. Rental apartments can also start low, around $80(USD), but will typically be more in the range of $250(USD) to $850(USD) a night. Some weekly rentals can cost $35,000(USD).

Packages and hotels that offer a significant number of amenities and services will usually come at a higher nightly rate. However, travelers may be able to save money with these packages if they plan to take advantage spa services, snorkeling, and scuba diving. Purchasing these amenities as part of your lodging package may be less expensive than buying them individually. Kitchens in rental properties allow travelers to save money by cooking rather than splurging on the island's fine cuisine.

Daily Spending

Next to lodging, food is the traveler's next major expense. Anguilla has a number of unpretentious bars and restaurants, as well as fast food establishments and barbecue stands. But many vacationers travel to the island to sample some of the Caribbean's finest cuisine at Anguilla's fanciest restaurants. Moderately priced restaurants have main courses that range from $15(USD) to $30(USD), but travelers can enjoy inexpensive meals from $5(USD) to $15(USD). Entrees in the island's nicest restaurants will run from $30(USD) to $50(USD), and three course meals in these establishments will quickly add up. Wine and drinks will also add considerable costs, and service charges may be included in the bill. Travelers should tip 15 to 20 percent.

Anguilla is just 16 miles long, but you'll need to factor transportation costs into your budget. There are no buses, but travelers can choose from rental cars, taxis, mopeds, and bikes. Rental cars give travelers the mobility and freedom to explore any of the island's 33 beaches at their leisure. Rental cars cost between $45(USD) and $70(USD) a day. A $20(USD) local license is needed to drive in Anguilla. Collision damage insurance can be as high as $15(USD) a day. Active vacationers can rent bikes or mopeds to explore the island. Bikes allow travelers to head off of the road to explore the flora and fauna of Anguilla, while mopeds allow more flexibility and mobility than a car on city streets. Average daily rental cost is $10(USD) for a bike and $27(USD) for a moped.

Visitors who will be doing limited touring of the island can consider hiring a taxi. Taxis are unmetered because rates are fixed and regulated. Although the frequent use of a taxi can quickly become expensive, a limited number of trips shared by several passengers are affordable. Taxi drivers also offer island tours. Taxi fares start as low as

$8(USD) and go as high as $22(USD). Taxi drivers should be tipped 10 percent. Day trips to St. Martin and St. Maarten gives travelers the opportunity to indulge in duty-free shopping. A ferry makes the journey from Blowing Point, Anguilla to Marigot, St. Martin for $10(USD) each way.

Another daily expense that can contribute to your overall budget is water sports and adventure activities. Single scuba dives can start as low as $45(USD), but these expenses will become significant if you are with a family or will be adventuring frequently.

Shopping

You will definitely want to set aside a bit of your budget for shopping, though you may not be doing much of it on Anguilla. While many Caribbean islands are filled with open air markets, clothing boutiques, and souvenir shops, shopping on Anguilla is limited to overpriced resort boutiques and designer stores. Luckily, a short ferry to neighboring St. Maarten and St. Martin is available to travelers who want to enjoy a few hours of duty-free shopping. St. Maarten/St. Martin is an especially popular shopping location for those interested in purchasing jewelry and watches, but designer duds, handmade crafts, and island apparel are also available. For those who prefer to stay local, a little extra searching will prove that there are several eclectic shops and art galleries off the beaten path. Locally produced rum is another popular item, and travelers can return to the United

States with up to two-liters of alcohol duty free. For more information on import and export duty, another factor you'll need to work into your budget, visit our guide to Customs section in this book.

Taxes

Hotel bills will include a 10 percent hotel tax on the bill in addition to any service charges. The departure tax if leaving by airplane or boat is $20 (USD) for adults, and $10 (USD) for children between the ages of five and 12.

While travelers are unlikely to spend large sums of money on shopping in Anguilla, the general cost of staying here can be expensive. Proper planning and budgeting can allow travelers to get the most out of their money on their dream vacation in the Caribbean.

Getting Info

How to Get the Info You Need for Your Trip to Anguilla
Anguilla stuns travelers with its numerous beautiful beaches
Anguilla, a relatively small strip of land on the outskirts of the Leewards Islands, gives Caribbean vacationers the opportunity to visit a safe and peaceful island with 33 resplendent white sand beaches. The more you learn about this dependent British territory, the more excited you will be to visit.

The process of vacation planning usually begins after you take the time to learn a bit about Anguilla. Often, all it takes is hearing about another person's experience in Anguilla to spark your interest. If you know someone who has traveled to Anguilla, do not fail to tap into this valuable resource of information. Friends, family, and business associates will be happy to give you insight and advice on traveling to the island, including what they enjoyed or disliked. Those who have already traveled to the island can give you advice on proper social conduct and recommendations for the perfect beach or restaurant. Additionally, you may be able to learn about places to avoid on your trip. Many who have visited Anguilla may feel a personal attachment to the island and will be more than happy to provide suggestions.

Would-be Caribbean travelers can browse through the travel section at their local bookstore. General Caribbean travel guides provide information on traveling to the region, as well as abbreviated information on specific islands. These general guides can be a good way to learn a little about the various islands as you decide which one to visit. There are also a number of travel guide books that exclusively cover particular islands. These guides provide in-depth reviews, information, and advice. Guides may focus on a particular type of traveler, so you should browse through several of them to decide which best suits you. You may also wish to purchase a guide to carry with you as a helpful resource during your trip.

Although books will be your primary resource in a bookstore, it can also be useful to browse through the magazine rack. Look for publications covering general travel interests or the Caribbean in particular. Travel magazines often have useful tips and advice for frequent travelers, and specific Caribbean-oriented magazines may have featured articles with ideas for vacation spots or activities. Magazines will also have a number of advertisements that can give travelers additional ideas and specific contact information.

Although these magazines may not always have articles that directly address Anguilla, they can be useful for general information. In order to find magazine articles dealing specifically with Anguilla, travelers may wish to make note of which magazines have Web sites. Magazine Web sites often archive their past articles in searchable databases, allowing Internet users to find relevant articles through a keyword search. To see if the magazine archives information on Anguilla, simply search for "Anguilla" or terms for particular hotels, beaches, or restaurants.

While friends and coworkers are a great starting point, and books and magazines can be helpful sources, the Internet is swiftly becoming one of the most popular ways of researching and booking a vacation. The proliferation of high speed Internet access has made looking for travel information even faster and more convenient from the comfort and privacy of your own home. There are a large number of sites of varying reliability covering travel to the Caribbean, and travelers can spend hours browsing through this huge collection of Web sites.

This Internet site strives to provide travelers with a comprehensive and detailed look at Anguilla. Information can be found on topics ranging from ferries and boats, to hotels and resorts, even telephones and postal services. Travelers can easily navigate through the clean interface to jump quickly to the information that interests them, or simply browse to learn a great deal about the island. Tourist office Web sites are additional sources of comprehensive information, and these sties provide official representation and information. Often, these sites will have up-to-date and breaking news concerning an island, along with general travel tips, accommodation information, and more. The Caribbean Tourism Organization Web site covers tourism industry related news and provides a calendar of events. The official site of the Anguilla Tourist Board can be a great contact if you need to ask a question about Anguilla.

There is still much left to explore in the expanses of the Internet, and travelers may next wish to turn to Internet vendor Web sites. Even if you are not ready to book your travel, many of these sites provide information on destinations. Their listings of hotels and tours can give you an idea of how to begin to plan, budget, and book your travel. In addition, there are also online yellow pages and business directories that travelers may consult for similar information. These sites may provide everything from phone numbers and addresses to direct links to other Internet sites for services and business in Anguilla. Travelers looking for contact information for hotels, restaurants, or tour and adventure operators may wish to consult these sites for an idea of what is available.

A final useful Internet source can be message and bulletin boards that cover travel to the Caribbean or Anguilla. These discussion forums allow both former and prospective travelers to convene and discuss the island. Former travelers can log on to provide information and opinions on experiences at particular beaches, hotels, restaurants, and sites, while prospective travelers can browse through past posts or ask a question of their own by creating a new post. Travelers must be cautious when consulting unofficial Internet sites and message and bulletin boards. These sources may not be reliable, even if their intention is genuine. Important information regarding travel and safety should be obtained only from official sources. Of equal importance, travelers should never disclose personal information to other Internet users.

By consulting a few sources on the Internet or in a bookstore, travelers will quickly find a world of information as they research a vacation to Anguilla.

Making Decisions
Need Help Making Decisions for Your Trip to Anguilla?

Travelers need to make several decisions as they plan their trip to Anguilla

The decision to travel to Anguilla can be quite an easy one. The island's pristine beaches and delightful food delight visitors' senses. But before departing, travelers must make important decisions about travel plans, hotel arrangements, and daily itineraries.

Travel

Travelers can make their way by air or sea to this small island in the north of the Leeward Islands. Wallblake Airport, located in the center of the island, is Anguilla's only airport and receives flights from other islands. Nonstop flights from the United States and Europe are not available, but travelers can easily connect to Anguilla via Puerto Rico to the east, or from other nearby islands including Antigua, St. Maarten, St. Thomas, and St. Kitts. Although a connecting flight is required, the ease and speed of air travel convinces many travelers to fly to Anguilla.

Cruises are another option for visiting Anguilla. Travelers can take small cruise lines to islands in the eastern Caribbean, including Anguilla. Nearby St. Maarten is one of the most popular cruise destinations in all of the Caribbean, and travelers can take a ferry from that island to Anguilla. Cruise travel and ferry day trips allow travelers to include Anguilla in their Caribbean travel without spending their entire vacation there.

Yachting facilities in Anguilla are limited, but sailors who are touring the Leeward Islands in the northern and eastern Caribbean can call on the quiet and scenic island.

Travelers have several options for touring Anguilla once they have arrived, including taxis, rental cars, bikes, and mopeds. For freedom and mobility, many travelers will choose rental cars. Fixed rate taxis are an option for travelers who will be doing less traveling, since costs can quickly add up if traveling to several locations in a day. Two-wheeled transportation may be ideal for adventurous travelers who want to see the countryside on a bike or zip around town on a scooter.

Visitors have a variety of transportation choices for getting to and around Anguilla. It's hard to go wrong as long as you get there. Still, travelers should consider their travel plans as they think about the vacation experience they would like to have.

Staying There

Although Anguilla is small, the island has quite a few hotels. Travelers can choose from a number of accommodation styles, from luxurious resorts to rental properties to small inns. Most accommodations are located in the southwest and northeast areas of the island. Beaches are concentrated in both of these areas, and dive sites are concentrated on the northeastern shore.

While all-inclusive resorts are appealing to many travelers, they are not prevalent on Anguilla. However, there are some hotels and resorts that offer package deals with lodging, meals, activities, spa and health services, and entertainment.

Travelers who value intimacy and quiet may choose to stay at a smaller guesthouse, inn, or rental villa. These accommodations allow travelers to escape the crowds of tourists. In particular, rental villas can provide complete privacy.

Activities and Sites

After choosing how to travel and where to stay, the most exciting part of the decision making process can be deciding what to do. There are a number of activities and attractions to enjoy in Anguilla, and travelers should explore anything that captures their interest.

The captivating beaches for which the island is known are a primary attraction, and travelers should take time to explore at least several of them during their stay. Good snorkeling can be enjoyed at a number of these beaches, and there are several dive sites along the northeast coast. The normal assortment of watersports are also available.

Travelers can take a day trip by ferry to St. Maarten, where the duty-free shopping outshines Anguilla's modest shops. Still, travelers can find crafts, art, fabrics, and even some luxury items on Anguilla.

The choices are yours as you plan your trip to Anguilla. With serene beaches and ample actives at your fingertips, it is hard to go wrong on this British Caribbean island.

Packing

Suggestions for Packing for a Vacation in Anguilla
Learn exactly what you need to get you through a vacation in Anguilla
If this is your first trip to the tropical island paradise of Anguilla, you may be wondering just exactly what to pack.

The great thing about Anguilla is that the year-round pleasant temperatures mean you don't have to pack in anticipation of unexpected shifts in weather. Still, every vacationer worries they will forget to pack something important – or that something they should pack isn't even on their radar. Taking into consideration local clothing customs and style sensibility is an important aspect to consider as well.

First and Foremost
Traveling to Anguilla requires that you arrive at the airport prepared with a few documents in hand. In order to enter the country, a current passport must be presented that is valid for at least six months after the date of travel. Some travelers will also be required to have a visa, but United States, Canada, and United Kingdom travelers are exempt.

You should have your passport on you at all times as you travel from home to Anguilla, and it would also be wise of you to make a photocopy and store it separately. This way, if your original passport is lost or stolen, you can bring the copy to an embassy or consulate for help.

Making sure you have enough money on hand to get you through your trip is important as well. Anguilla visitors often use credit cards to make purchases, but having cash on hand is just as important in case a situation arises in which you need it (such as a credit card machine being down). The official currency in Anguilla is the Eastern Caribbean Dollar, and you can exchange your money when you arrive on the island at the airport, in a bank, or at an ATM.

If you are taking any prescription medications, make sure to have these on hand along with a note from your physician regarding your health issues and need for the medication..

Finally, you will not want to misplace any of the following documents: airline tickets, hotel confirmation, rental vehicle confirmation, and paperwork detailing any excursions and activities you have arranged ahead of time. To help you remember everything you will need, we have a assembled an Important Documents and Money checklist that you can use.

Clothing

When you are thinking about the items you'll be bringing with you, consider the activities you'll be participating in. While touring the island you will be most comfortable in light-weight clothing that will keep you cool and won't become heavy and uncomfortable as the day goes on. Keep in mind that light-colored clothing will not absorb the sunlight as much as darks will. Cotton and linen t-shirts and tank tops are the best option for your top half, and shorts and khaki pants are ideal for bottoms. Dresses and skirts should be saved for outings that require little activity, such as a museum tour or dinner. Comfortable athletic shoes or hiking shoes are best as you explore Anguilla.

A few items you won't want to overlook include enough pairs of under garments and socks to make it through the trip and a pair of pajamas.

Formal Wear

Formal wear is not absolutely necessary. You can get away with spending your whole vacation in shorts and t-shirts if you stick to the type of environment that those items are appropriate. However, if you plan to have a night out at a classy restaurant, you will want to dress the part. Collared shirts and slacks for men, and sun dresses, skirts, or slacks and a blouse for women will do the trip. Know your venue. In some cases, you may even want to done a business suit and a cocktail dress, but this is something you can plan for in advance. Make sure to bring the appropriate shoes for each outfit as well.

Swim Wear

When vacationing in Anguilla, you will need at least one swimsuit, and many people prefer to bring two. This way, you can wear one while the other one is hanging to dry from water activities the previous day. It will also give you options.

It is advisable that you bring a cover-up so that you can go from the sand to the streets with little fuss, and avoid offending island sensibilities by walking into a shop wearing just your suit. And you definitely do not want to forget a hat, your sunglasses, a pair of sandals or flip flops to protect your feet from the hot sand.

Toiletries and Health Care

Bathroom items that you use on a regular basis, such as a toothbrush, toothpaste, hair care products, and deodorant should be brought with you if you don't want to use the brands that your hotel will likely provide you with. You can buy any item you would like to bring with you to Anguilla in travel sizes so that they do not take up any extra space, but if you plan to do this, do it before you travel. Buying your toiletries back home will be less expensive than the hotel gift shop, where prices are often marked up - so save a buck and make sure to pack some of these items

It is doubly important that you remember to bring with you any prescription medication, as long as well as your prescription slip or a note from your doctor. Don't forget our Medication and Health Items checklist when packing.

Mosquitoes and sand fleas are common in Anguilla, and it is important that you protect yourself from these vermin. Bring along insect repellant to apply to your body before you leave your hotel, as well as periodically throughout the day. If you are unfortunate enough to be bit, hydrocortisone cream or Benadryl will reduce the itchiness.

What Else to Pack

The days are hot in Anguilla, but some nights can get colol as well. If you plan to spend time outside at night, you should pack a sweater or wrap. Although Anguilla experiences limited rainfall, you should bring a poncho, rain jacket, or umbrella to keep you dry when drops do fall. Don't forget the appropriate exercise clothing if you plan to hit the gym.

Comfort items and entertainment should not be overlooked. You will likely have some down time, and will certainly be spending a good amount of time traveling, so having these things with you will help curb your boredom. Suggestions include a book or your e-reader, an mp3 player, a portable DVD player, a personal journal, a laptop, and a hand held video game system. Batteries and power cords to keep these devises up and running are important as well.

Most importantly for many vacationers is their camera. Don't forget to pack your camera and all of the equipment you need to keep it up and running, plus an extra memory card.

Packing Concerns

A great way to save space when packing for your trip to Anguilla is to plan several outfits that include interchangeable clothing. Choose items that can be worn in a few different ways while still appearing fresh and clean. For example, a pair of cloth shorts will pair with a variety of shirts, and a selection of colored shirts can be layered differently on each day of your trip for a new look.

One concern that a lot of travelers face is the thought that their luggage might get lost or delayed by the airline when they fly to Anguilla. This is rare, but if it does happen you don't have to be caught unprepared. Include one outfit and a swimsuit in your carry on luggage, and you will have enough to get you through until your luggage is found or you have a chance to purchase something new. You should also keep any important medications and small valuables in your carry on. Don't let packing for your Anguilla vacation overwhelm you. By using the above list as a guideline, you will be sure to have everything you need to make you feel at home while on vacation.

Best Time to Visit

When is the Best Time to Visit Anguilla?

There are two distinct seasons for travel in the Caribbean

When cooler temperatures begin to nip at residents of North America and Europe, many travelers choose to make the Caribbean their vacation destination. Although winter is the most popular travel season in the Caribbean, there can be distinct benefits to traveling during the off-season.

The lushly adorned landscapes, the clean sandy beaches, and the invigorating blue waters make traveling to Anguilla an appealing option throughout the year. However, frigid temperatures in other areas of the world seems to spur travelers to visit the island during the popular Caribbean tourist season of mid-December to mid-April.

Weather

The average yearly temperature in Anguilla is 80 degrees Fahrenheit, with only slight variations in the warmer or cooler periods. The island is relatively dry, with just 35 inches of annual rainfall. The rainy season in Anguilla occurs during the summer and fall hurricane months. Hurricane season in the Atlantic lasts from the beginning of June until the end of November, and these menacing Atlantic storm systems keep many travelers from visiting the region during this time. Anguilla, located in the north of the Leeward Islands, is subject to frequent Atlantic tropical storms and hurricanes.

Anguilla's Off-Season

Despite the threat of hurricanes and increased rainfall, the summer months can still be a pleasant time to visit the island. With its northern position in the Caribbean, trade winds keep the island's summer temperatures mild and enjoyable. Summer can also be better for scuba divers, as water visibility is at its highest. The off-season in the Caribbean, from the middle of April to the middle of December, does offer travelers significant savings on air travel and accommodations, with prices being slashed up to 50 percent. Crowds will decrease significantly during this time, meaning that travelers may find it easier to find that secluded beach or secure a dinner reservation. Travelers who decide to travel during this time period should keep a watchful eye on Atlantic storm developments prior to and during their trip.

Travelers should also be aware that many hotels and restaurants may curtail their hours or shut down for weeks or months at a time during this period. Recreation vendors may also limit their services. With the number of tourists on the island so low, many hotels will use the off season to conduct repairs and renovation of their properties. In order to avoid staying in a construction zone, travelers should check with hotels to determine what types of construction will be going on and how it is expected to impact visitors.

Hotels and restaurants that are under construction during this time period are readying themselves for the busy tourist season when these services will rise to meet the higher demand of travelers. Hotels and restaurants will be newly renovated and fully staffed to provide the highest quality of customer attention and care. The influx of vacationers and day trippers from St. Maarten will mean that recreation and adventure services will be running at full capacity. Because these winter months are so popular, flights and hotels are booked months in advance. This is especially true at the nicer resorts. Travelers looking to vacation in Anguilla during the tourist season should make their reservations far in advance. Since the island is known for its cuisine, restaurant reservations are essential even during the winter months.

Events and Festivals

A number of festivals and holidays take place in Anguilla, and travelers should take advantage of the opportunity to experience some local culture. Late February brings the Moonsplash Annual Music Festivalwith international talent, and the relatively new Annual Jazz Festivaloccurs only a few weeks later in the middle of March. A second jazz festival, the Tranquility Jazz Festival, takes place in the second week of November. The Anguilla Annual Yacht Regatta is held in early May, while a boat race is also held in celebration of Easter. Carnival, during the first part of August, includes the traditional pageantry and excitement of the festival.

There are benefits to vacationing during both the high and low travel seasons in Anguilla. This is lucky for vacationers who don't have much choice in when their vacation takes place. Travelers in complete control of their trip have a much harder choice to make, but should take comfort in knowing that Anguilla will rise up to greet them regardless of when they choose to go.

Transportation

Anguilla Transportation Options

Anguilla is a small island in the north of the Leeward Islands

Situated just north of the significantly busier St. Maarten, Anguilla is a quiet island paradise that awes its visitors with some of the finest beaches in the Caribbean. Although this destination is not as accessible as other Caribbean islands, the journey is certainly worth the effort.

Air Travel

Although arrival options include both air and sea, many travelers choose to travel to Anguilla by air. Indeed, visitors traveling from Europe and much of North America have few other options. Clayton Lloyd International Airport (formerly the Wallblake Airport), located in the center of the island, receives air traffic from neighboring Caribbean islands, but does not receive planes traveling directly from North America or Europe. Travelers from these locations must make connections on islands such as Puerto Rico and Sint Maarten in order to reach Anguilla. Most tourists can stay on the island for up to three months without a visa. Read on Air Travel page in this book to learn more about air travel in Anguilla.

Sailing

Sailing is the final option for traveling to Anguilla and can be perfect for adventurous and independent travelers. The island has two ports of entry, Blowing Point and Road Bay, and several beautiful offshore islands. Inexperienced sailors can charter boats that have fully trained crews, while seasoned seafarers can charter a boat to sail by themselves. Regardless of experience, however, sailors should be careful of rough waters and strong trade winds. Sailing in the Leeward Islands is popular, with a number of fabled ports and islands to welcome travelers. The quiet beauty of Anguilla is sure to please sailors who anchor here. Learn more about the ins and outs of sailing to the island by reading our Sailing and Boating page in this book.

Cruises

Caribbean cruises allow travelers to see Anguilla while also experiencing several other islands, such as Jost Van Dyke or Guadeloupe. Travelers who want to visit Anguilla, but who would also like to visit destinations that have more opportunities for shopping and other activities, may wish to travel by cruise. While Sint Maarten to the south is a bustling cruise port, Anguilla does not see a large number of cruise vessels call at Blowing Point. Vessels that do travel to the island tend to be smaller and provide travelers with luxury cruise experiences. Upon disembarking, cruise passengers can visit one of the island's many beaches or sample some of the fine international cuisine.

Although Anguilla is under the radar of many Caribbean tourists, travelers who do make their way to the island will have the memory of its stunning beaches etched into their minds. Find out more about your cruising options read on Cruises page in this book.

Rental Cars

Families and groups of three or four who plan to do a substantial amount of traveling on Anguilla may find that rental cars are the most cost efficient method of transportation. Both international and local car rental firms rent vans, jeeps, and cars. Drivers must have a valid driver's license from their home country along with a local driver's permit that costs $20(USD). driving is done on the left hand side of the road in Anguilla.

If you do plan on renting a car on the island, it is suggested that you read our Anguilla Rental Car page in this book.

Bikes and Mopeds

Anguilla is not as mountainous as some other Caribbean islands, which makes bikes and mopeds more feasible options for travelers looking for freedom and adventure. Traveling by mountain bike allows you to discover the flora and fauna along island trails. Bikes are also good for a quick ride from your hotel to the beach. Scooters and mopeds allow travelers to explore the island's cities and beaches on a whim and can help them save money on gas. Be especially careful when riding bikes and mopeds on the island's rugged roads.

Taxis

Taxis are available throughout the island for transportation and tours. Fares are fixed by the government, although multiple travelers and luggage can incur additional fees. Taxi rates can add up quickly, but travelers who are doing a limited amount of touring should consider this option. Speaking of touring, one of the great things about taxi drivers on Anguilla is that they are also often trained tour guides as well. For a nominal fee (starting at around $40 a day), you can hire your taxi driver to take you on a tour of the island. Don't plan on this as your official means of getting to know Anguilla, but if you happen upon an amiable driver, you may get a better tour out of him or her than an official touring company. Read on Taxis page in this book to find out more.

Buses

As a result of the island's small size, there is no public transportation on Anguilla. That does not mean, however, that bus transportation is out of the question. Harry's Taxi and Tour Bus Service rents out buses to large groups for transportation and island tours. These buses can hold anywhere from 15 to 45 passengers, and are popular amongst large groups that travel to the island together, such as wedding parties and school trippers. You can find out more information in Buses page in this book.

Ferries

Finally, travelers who wish to take a day trip to Sint Maarten for the more alluring duty-free shopping opportunities can take a ferry from Blowing Point in Anguilla to Marigot in St. Martin. Travelers must pay a fare and departure tax and should carry their passport. Even with these fees, most travelers agree that a trip betwen the two islands is not one that should be missed. How often would you get a chance to visit two countries with such different cultural backgrounds in the span of just one day? Read our Anguilla Ferry page in this book for additional information.

Despite the lack of public transportation, there are a number of ways to explore Anguilla, and every one of them is considered to be safe and inexpensive by Caribbean islands standards. Whichever method you feel most comfortable with, be it taking matters into your own hands with a rental, or hiring a charted bus for a large group of people, you'll find that all roads (and waterways) lead to adventure.

Air Travel

How to Reach Anguilla by Airplane

Travelers must take connecting flights in order to reach Anguilla

With the expansive Atlantic Ocean separating travelers from the Caribbean Sea, most people opt to use air travel to reach Anguilla. Although flying is convenient and quick, foreign travelers are required to first fly to a neighboring Caribbean island before heading to Anguilla.

Flying to Anguilla from the US

Travelers in the United States typically fly American Airlines to San Juan before taking a short one-hour flight to Anguilla. As for getting to Puerto Rico, that will be easy. Air Transportation to Puerto Rico is common from the US, with several cities offering daily flights. The only tough decision you will have to make is if you want to spend some time in Puerto Rico or get to Anguilla as soon as possible.

Rumor has it that direct flights from major United States cities such as Atlanta and Miami are in the works, though some renovations may need to be made, since the 5463 foot runways is not long enough to receive international jets.

Flying to Anguilla from Europe

Travelers from Europe and other destinations around the world must connect in the United States or take a direct flight to a neighboring island. Depending what nation you are flying from, this usually includes Puerto Rico, Sint Maarten, or the the Dominican Republic.

You will be able to find flights to the Caribbean from Europe on board popular airlines like British Airways, Virgin Airlines, Condor Airlines, and several others.

Flying to Anguilla from the Caribbean

The main airport in Anguilla is the Clayton Lloyd International Airport, which you can contact at 264-498-5922. Once known as the Wallblake Airport, this locale was renamed in 2010. It is a small terminal with no jet ways, and is located in the center of the island, just south of The Valley. The airport receives as many as 50 inter-island flights daily from locations such as San Juan, Sint Maarten, Antigua, and St. Kitts.

See below for scheduled air service from other Caribbean airports. Even if you can't take a flight from an airport near your home, connecting through another airport in the Caribbean might be a viable solution.

Clayton Lloyd International Airport Caribbean Flights

To/From	Airport Code	Airlines
Antigua, Antigua and Barbuda	ANU	Air St. Maarten, LIAT
Basseterre, St. Kitts	SKB	Winair
Gustavia, St. Barthelemy	SBH	Anguilla Air Services
Isla Verde, Puerto Rico	SJU	American Airlines, Cape Air, United Airlines

Nevis, Saint Kitts and Nevis	NEV	Winair
Saba	SAB	Winair
Simpson Bay, The island of St. Martin and Sint Maarten	SXM	Anguilla Air Services
St. Eustatius, Saint Eustatius	EUX	Winair
St. Thomas, US Virgin Islands	STT	LIAT
the BVI, British Virgin Islands	EIS	Winair
the Dominican Republic	SDQ	Winair

Flying to the Caribbean can be expensive, however there are several ways to save money on flights. Since there are no non-stop flights from foreign destinations to Anguilla, travelers should search for a number of connecting islands and flights in order to get the best deal. Flying during the slow tourist season in the Caribbean can save travelers up to 50 percent on airfare and hotels. Airlines also sometimes release last minute deals. Return tickets can be less expensive than two one-way tickets. Advance booking, reward programs, and frequent flier mile clubs are other ways to benefit and save on your travels.

Airport Security

As a result of safety concerns, airports and airlines have increased their security measures. Luggage checks and searches have become more thorough, and travelers must move through several check points when taking their flight to the Caribbean. Although increased security has caused some delays and heavier airport traffic, security officials have streamlined the process as much as possible, and air travelers realize that the measures have been implemented for their own safety. Vacationers can contact the Transportation Security Administration (http://www.tsa.gov) (TSA) at 866-289-9673 with questions concerning baggage screening and security concerns, as well as for a full list of prohibited items.

Passengers can take several measures to ensure that they get to their flight quickly and without complications. The first important step is confirming your flight. Call the airline a few days in advance to confirm the flight times, flight number, and ticket assignments. Arrive at the airport two hours before your flight is scheduled to depart in case of delays or unseen complications at the ticketing counter or security checkpoints. The popularity of electronic tickets has prompted the spread of electronic ticket kiosks where passengers can quickly print their boarding passes. In order to move through all of the checkpoints, travelers should have a valid government issued photo ID (passport) and a boarding pass.

Once past ticketing, travelers are likely to experience the most delays as they wait to move through the primary passenger screening area that allows entrance to the airport terminals. Items such as razors, scissors, and other sharp objects are not allowed through these checkpoints. Consult the TSA (http://www.tsa.gov) for a complete list of restricted items.

Prepare to move through the security checkpoint by removing any bulky metallic items such as belt buckles, steel boots, and jewelry. Additionally, remove all jackets, coats, and blazers. Passengers are also required to remove shoes and hats. Computers and camcorders must be taken out of their cases in order to be sent through the baggage screening machine, and they may be closely inspected. Personal valuables, such as cell phones, PDAs, loose change and jewelry should be placed in the bins provided by the airport when moving through the security checkpoint. Travelers with pacemakers or metal surgical implants should speak with airport security officials in order to make arrangements for security screening.

Airlines generally allow one carry-on item and one personal item such as a purse, briefcase, or laptop computer. Airlines have different rules for checked baggage and may charge fees for items such as golf clubs, so it is best to contact the specific airline directly.

Air Charters

Charter flights are another way you can fly into Anguilla. More personalized and flying on your schedule, chartering a plan can help you get to islands much easier than having to find a scheduled flight. Generally, flights aboard charter planes are a little longer than with airlines, since the planes go slower. However, there are also less procedures and regulations before takeoff, so no need to get there hours ahead of time.

Take a look at the chart below for some charters that are based around Anguilla. Many specialize in one service or another, so be sure to call and ask.

Take a look at this next chart if you want to get in touch with some of the regional air charter companies.

Charter Operators			
Name	Phone	Location	Island
Epelem Flying Services	(721) 544-5240	Princess Juliana International Airport - 1.0 mi. (1.7 km) West-Northwest of Simpson Bay	the island of St. Martin and Sint Maarten
Fly BVI Pickup Service from NGD	(284) 495-1747	Auguste George Airport - Anegada	Anegada
Fly BVI Pickup Service from SXM	(284) 495-1747	Princess Juliana International Airport - 1.0 mi. (1.7 km) West-Northwest of Simpson Bay	the island of St. Martin and Sint Maarten
Melmik Aviation	(721) 547-0725	Princess Juliana International Airport - 1.0 mi. (1.7 km) West-Northwest of Simpson Bay	the island of St. Martin and Sint Maarten
Menzies Avation Group	(721) 545-2570	Princess Juliana International Airport - 1.0 mi. (1.7 km) West-	the island of St. Martin and Sint

		Northwest of Simpson Bay	Maarten
Shoreline Aviation at North Sound	(340) 642-3000	5.9 mi. (9.6 km) Northeast of Spanish Town	Virgin Gorda
St. Barth Commuter	(590) 590 27 54 54	Gustaf III Airport - St. Barthelemy	St. Barthelemy

Although you may need to take a connecting flight to travel to Anguilla, flying remains the quickest and most convenient way to reach this beautiful island.

Buses

Are there Buses for Tourists in Anguilla?
The small island does not have a public bus transportation system
Anguilla is a small island in the northern Leeward Islands, just 16 miles long and 3 miles wide. With such a small land area and a modest amount of yearly visitors, there is little justification for a public bus service.

Since Anguilla is so small, travelers are never far away from any of the island's beaches and restaurants. Guests can choose from several options when they do need to travel around the island.

Although it is not public transportation, there is one bus service on the island that can be rented by groups of travelers. Harry's Taxi and Tour

Bus Service (264-497-4336) charters buses that can hold anywhere from 15 to 45 passengers for day tours and excursions.

Vacationers who will be doing a limited amount of traveling around the island can utilize the government regulated taxi services. Rates are based on two passengers, and splitting the cost of the fare can help to save money. Taxi fares can quickly add up, however, and travelers who will be traveling frequently in Anguilla are recommended to secure a rental car from one of the many agencies on the island. Drivers need a temporary local license, and driving is done on the left hand side of the road.

Scooters and bikes are good options for independent and athletic travelers. Anguilla does not have the hilly terrain that many of the Caribbean islands do, making it more suitable for two-wheel travel. Travelers on bikes and mopeds must exercise caution if on the road, but letting the salty ocean air whisk by as you travel from beach to beach can be an exhilarating and memorable experience.

Travelers should not be put off by the lack of buses in Anguilla, as there are a number of other good ways to travel from place to place.

Ferries

Take a ferry ride to neighboring islands for an exciting day trip

Taking the ferry is a unique and charming way to navigate Anguilla's waterways and visit neighboring islands. Planning a day trip to nearby St. Martin is no problem at all with the frequent ferry services from Anguilla. This little tropical island is a great place to explore the wonders of the Caribbean.

Riding the Ferries

Vacationers don't need to make reservations to catch a ride on any of the island's fantastic ferries. All you have to do to take the ferry from Anguilla to Sint Maarten is put your name and passport number on the manifest at the pier as soon as you get there. You'll pay a departure tax of $5 and a security fee of $3(USD) on top of the fee for riding aboard the ferry, and then you're all set. You can also charter ferry boats for your own personal inter-island excursions. For more information on chartered sailing, visit our guide to Anguilla Sailing and Boating page in this book.

Make finding water transportation easy by browsing the selection of ferry services below.

Ferry Docks

Name	Phone	Location	Island
Blowing Point Ferry Terminal	--	South End of Main Road - 0.4 mi. (0.6 km) South of Blowing Point	Anguilla
Cul de Sac Ferry	--	French Cul-de-Sac	the island of St. Martin and Sint

Dock			Maarten
Fort St. Louis Dock	(059) 051-1111	Downtown Marigot	the island of St. Martin and Sint Maarten
Marigot Ferry Port	--	Downtown Marigot	the island of St. Martin and Sint Maarten
Pinel Island Ferry Dock	--	1.3 mi. (2.1 km) North of Orient Bay	the island of St. Martin and Sint Maarten

Rate and Schedules

Ferries are operated by independent boat owners, and a public ferry from St. Martin is scheduled to run approximately every forty-five minutes from 7:00 a.m. to 7:00 p.m. between Blowing Point, Anguilla and Marigot, St. Martin. The trips take approximately 20 minutes, and is quite reasonably priced at $15(USD), in addition to the departure and security tax. When returning to Anguilla from St. Martin you will need to pay this fare once again, as well as a $5(USD) departure fee.

Blowing Point Ferry - Regular Schedule	
To St. Maarten	To Anguilla
7:30 am	8:15 am
8:15 am	9:00 am

9:00 am	9:45 am
9:45 am	10:30 am
10:30 am	11:15 am
11:15 am	12:45 pm
12:00 pm	1:30 pm
12:45 pm	2:15 pm
1:30 pm	3:00 pm
2:15 pm	3:45 pm
3:00 pm	4:30 pm
3:45 pm	5:15 pm
4:30 pm	6:00 pm
5:15 pm	7:00 pm
6:15 pm	

Once you have purchased your ferry ticket, make sure that all of your luggage is close at hand to prevent your bags from being lost or stolen. Always keep your passport in a secure and handy location. It will be checked before you leave the port, as you are traveling to a different country. Once the captain has made the announcement, you can begin to board the ferry. These ferries do not carry vehicles between the islands.

Planning a ferry ride during your vacation on Anguilla is great way to experience the smaller neighboring islands, which may be more easily accessed by boat than other means of transportation.

Ferry Routes, Anguilla

Location Served	Dock A	Dock B	Company	Frequency
Blowing Point	Fort St. Louis Dock	Blowing Point Ferry Terminal	Public Ferry	many times per day
Blowing Point	Philipsburg Ferry Dock	Blowing Point Ferry Terminal	Link Cat Ferry Service	several times per day
Blowing Point	Simpson Bay Ferry Port	Blowing Point Ferry Terminal	Anguilla Ferry and Charter Service	many times per day

Rental Cars

Car Rentals in Anguilla

Rental cars allow travelers to easily and quickly get from place to place in Anguilla

Although the traffic moves relatively slowly on Anguilla, the island is only 16 miles long, so getting from place to place will never take very long. Travelers who want the freedom and mobility to explore the island's 33 beaches at their own pace should consider a rental car.

Renting a Car

Several international car rental agencies, including Avis and Thrifty Car Rental, are present on the island. Travelers can also choose from a number of local firms.

The table below lists the rental agencies located in the immediate vicinity of Anguilla.

Vehicle Rental Companies

Name	Phone	Location
Andy's Auto Rental	(264) 584-7010	Blowing Point Ferry Terminal - 0.4 mi. (0.6 km) South of Blowing Point
Anguilla Motors Ltd	(264) 497-2723	Airport Road - Stoney Ground
Avis Anguilla	(264) 497-2642	The Quarter
Bass Car Rental	(264) 497-2361	Farrington
Bryan's Car Rentals	(203) 992-5407	Blowing Point
Freeway Car Rental	(264) 497-6621	George Hill
Hertz Triple K Car Rental	(264) 497-2934	Airport Road - The Valley
High-Way Rent-A-Car	(264) 497-2183	George Hill

Island Car Rentals	(264) 497-2723	Airport Road - Stoney Ground
Junie's Car Rental	(264) 584-3720	0.4 mi. (0.6 km) South of Blowing Point
Pete's Car Rental	(264) 497-6296	South Hill
Richardson's Car Rental Agency	(264) 498-8900	Rendezvous Bay
Romcan Car Rental	(264) 497-6265	South Hill
Summerset Car Rental	(264) 497-5278	George Hill
Thrifty Anguilla Airport	(264) 497-2656	Clayton Lloyd International Airport - The Valley
Wendell Connor's Car Rentals	(264) 497-6894	Blowing Point

Visitors who wish to drive on Anguilla must have a valid driver's license from their home country. Many rental firms require drivers to be at least 25 years of age. In addition, drivers must obtain a $20(USD) local driver's permit, issued by most of the island's car rental firms.

Requirements and restrictions can vary. If you are concerned about minimum and maximum age restrictions, insurance requirements and the like, consider contacting each firm directly, before making a final decision.

The Cost of Renting a Car

Jeeps, cars, and vans are all available, with rates ranging from $45(USD) to $70(USD) a day. Travelers must also purchase collision damage insurance, which ranges from $5(USD) to $15(USD) a day. Most firms allow for unlimited mileage, provide free pick up and delivery, and accept major credit cards.

Driving in Anguilla

Driving is done on the left hand side of the road in Anguilla. Drivers who are not accustomed to this traffic pattern should exercise additional caution when taking to the road. The speed limit throughout the island is 30 mph, except in towns and school zones where it is no more than 20 mph. Paved roads on the island can be in poor condition, with ruts and dips in the narrow lanes. Pay special attention to speed bumps and traffic roundabouts, and beware of goats, children, and pedestrians on the road, especially in the evenings. Always use caution and attentive driving skills when driving in a foreign country. You can read even more about driving on the island, read on our Driving page in this boook.

Gasoline stations in and around Anguilla are quite abundant. Be sure to check the list below for some of their locations. the chart

Gas stations

Name	Phone	Location
Albert Lake Shell Station	(264) 497-2240	Mahogany Tree Corner - The Valley
Anguilla Gas Station	(264) 497-6334	Main Road across from Bennies - Blowing Point
Delta Petroleum	(264) 497-5777	Long Path Road next to Tropical Flower - 2.4 mi. (3.9 km) East of the Valley
Delta Station	--	Across the street from Apex Auto Parts - The Valley
J & B Gas Services	(264) 497-2610	Long Ground Road - Stoney Ground
Smitty's Shell Gas	(264) 497-4300	Next to the Marina - Island Harbour
West End Shell Station	(264) 497-8020	Cove Road - West End Village

Most rental car services will not provide booster seats or car seats, so remember, if you are traveling with a young child you should bring a safety restraint system from home.

Whether you're looking to visit the West End Bay or Island Harbour, a rental car can quickly get you to any destination on Anguilla.

Sailing & Boating

Sailing and Boating Near Anguilla
Sailing and yachting are great ways to enjoy your island vacation
In addition to being one of Anguilla's most popular island pastimes, sailing is the island's national sport. Many vacationers enjoy participating in or simply observing this exciting water sport. The tradition of sailboat racing started years ago, when Anguillans returned from fishing trips and raced their boats home. From then on, the spirit of competition took over and created what is now the most popular sport in the Caribbean.

Anguilla hosts a number of annual sailboat racing events. Anguillans from around the world travel back home to the island just to be a part of these exciting events, which can be compared to mega-sporting events like the Super Bowl or World Cup. The racing season runs from May through August, so vacationers can join the locals as spectators from cliffside vantage points. These prized races are followed by post-race parties that can last into the wee hours of the night.

Some sailors and boaters are attracted to Anguilla's isolation, as well as the delightful bays on both the north and south coasts of the island. Boaters who seek some of the most private waters around Anguilla will discover heavenly solitude in the waters of the Prickly Pear Cays and Dog Island, which are just north of Anguilla. After clearing immigration, boaters can dock at Blowing Point and Road Bay, the island's main ports of entry. Be sure to clear your boat or yacht through customs properly; failure to do so could result in hefty fines or even confiscation of your vessel.

If you're simply wanting to enjoy a few hours on the open water, without the cost and responsibility associated with renting a boat you can take an excursion. Take a look at the table that follows for information on area excursion services.

Boat Excursions

Name	Phone	Location
Calypso Charters	(246) 584-8504	Docks at Blowing Point - 0.4 mi. (0.6 km) South of Blowing Point
Garfield's Sea Tours - Gotcha!	(264) 497-2956	Sandy Ground Village
Junior's Glass Bottom Boat	(264) 235-1008	Shoal Bay East
Sail Chocolat	(264) 497-3394	The Valley
Sea Pro Charters	(264) 584-0074	Sandy Ground Village

Boat Rentals and Charters

Travelers can choose from two different divisions of charter companies when deciding on a charter. The first way to classify a charter company is by size. First time yacht charterers should opt for a larger charter company for several reasons. First of all, large companies offer more guarantees and will replace your boat at no extra charge if a particular charter suddenly becomes unavailable. Smaller charter companies keep their organizations small in order to provide better customer service.

Charter companies can also be classified as either first or second tier. These classifications are not related to quality standards, but rather to the age of their boats. First tier charter companies have the newest boats, stocked with the most modern equipment and technologies, like cellular phones and CD players. First tier boats are usually no more than 4 or 5 years old. Second tier companies have older boats, which they usually purchase from first tier companies. These older boats cost less than newer boats, but generally do not have all of the extras of first tier boats.

It is important to find a crew that is compatible with you and your travel expectations when chartering a crewed boat. Charter brokers are a good way to find a suitable crew. Brokers are also an excellent way to find the best charter rates on bare boats and skippered charters. You don't have to worry about the cost of the broker because the charter company pays for their services.

Seriously considering a yacht or boat charter? The following chart enables you to reach a local charter company.

Charter And Rental Services

Name	Phone	Location
Fun Seaker	590 690 66-3395	Anguilla
Funtime Charters	(866) 334-0047	Anguilla
Nature Boy Charters	(264) 729-5587	Shoal Bay West
Tradition Sailing Charters	(264) 476-7245	Sandy Ground Village

Making a well-informed decision when chartering a yacht means considering your personal charter needs. The kind of yacht you charter will play a big part in the kind of vacation you will have. Here are some things to consider when deciding what kind of yacht to charter:

➢ For the most comfort on your charter, go with a yacht that has one more cabin than you anticipate using. Families may want to consider chartering a catamaran because they have the most comfortable cabins, experience less roll than other vessels, and are generally safer for children.

➢ The most popular bareboat charters are monohull yachts with three cabins and two bathrooms. These vessels range from about 36 to 50 feet in length. The drawback to these boats is that they have ply-wood walls, which carry sound very easily.

➢ If you charter a large ship with a lot of extra amenities, expect to pay more for your charter.

➢ Boats with canvases over the cockpit provide protection from the harsh rays of the sun.

➢ When chartering a bareboat, don't expect a lot of extras like kayaks or electronic gadgets. If you want these items, inquire ahead about their availability.

Docking

Sailors and boaters should always be cautious when navigating the waters of the Caribbean. Look out for coral reefs, especially around the island, which can do serious damage to your watercraft. Also, stay alert for unfavorable trade winds and storms that could be brewing over the water.

While sailing and boating, consider the ocean currents, which are considerably stronger in the Atlantic Ocean than in the waters of the Caribbean Sea. The season during which sail will also play a part in the conditions of the water. Hurricane season and heavy rains occur during the summer months, and less experienced boaters should avoid these sailing conditions.

Planning to reach Anguilla using your own vessel, or one you charter in a different location? See the listing below to find information concerning area marinas.

Marinas

Name	Phone	Location	Island
Docks at Blowing Point	--	0.4 mi. (0.6 km) South of Blowing Point	Anguilla

Enjoy the beautiful waters of Anguilla on an exciting charter trip that's sure to create lasting memories of this beautiful paradise.

Nearby Anchorages

Location	Latitude	Longitude
1.2 mi. (1.9 km) West of the Valley	18.2190598858	-63.0701065063
Sandy Ground Village	18.2010713138	-63.0918431282
Scrub Bay - Scrub Island	18.2819568564	-62.957990159

Taxis

Taxis provide transportation and guided tours for your island getaway

Catching a cab is a good way to see the island of Anguilla. Taxi drivers can be both your driver and your island tour guide. Once you get to Anguilla you should be able to find a cab with relative ease, as they meet all incoming flights. Unlike many other islands in the Caribbean, Anguilla's roads are in fairly good condition, so you won't experience as many bumps and potholes.

Take a look at the following chart for cab companies that serve Anguilla.

Taxi Services

Name	Phone	Location
Airport Taxi Stand	(264) 497-5054	Clayton Lloyd International Airport - The Valley
Blowing Point Taxi Stand	(264) 497-6089	Blowing Point Ferry Terminal - Blowing Point
Island Transport Services Ltd	(264) 497-2679	Stoney Ground
Premier Taxi & Tours	(264) 497-0515	The Valley

Rates, Fares, and Fees

Although cab fares on Anguilla are based on set rates, and the official fares are published in annual tourist guides, cab fares are unmetered. Therefore, it is wise to confirm the price of the ride with the driver before setting out on your journey. If you're traveling with a lot of luggage or need to make additional stops, inquire about additional charges. There is generally a $0.50(USD) surcharge per bag for more than two bags. Passengers must pay the cab fare in cash. Both U.S. dollars and Eastern Caribbean dollars are acceptable forms of payment. Two-hour island tours start at about $40(USD) for one or two people, with an additional $5(USD) charge for each additional passenger up to a maximum of six people.

The following charts show some of the average fares from several destinations around the island, including the airport and popular accommodations. Traveling in the island's more remote locations may incur extra costs.

Taxi Rates From Blowing Point Ferry	
Destination	Rates (in U.S. dollars)
Alamanda	$16.00
Blue Waters	$20.00
Frangipani Hotel	$18.00
Inter Island Hotel	$8.00
Mariners/Sandy Ground	$12.00
North Hill	$11.00
Pond Ground	$18.00
Sea Rocks	$22.00
Skiffles Villas	$10.00
Serenity Restaurant	$16.00
Cinnamon Reef Hotel	$14.00
Sea Horse Apt.	$8.00

Taxi Rates From Airport	
Destination	Rates (in U.S. dollars)
Blowing Point Cove	$14.00

Alamanda	$13.00
B/P Beach Apts.	$12.00
Sonesta	$20.00
Cap Juluca Hotel	$20.00
Caribella Hotel	$20.00
Casa Nadine	$6.00
Carimar Hotel	$16.00
Cocolobo Hotel	$18.00
Cul-De-Sac	$14.00
Corito Hotel	$10.00
Emerald Estate	$10.00
Sea Feathers	$12.00
Roys Restaurant	$8.00

Remember that if you are traveling with a small child you will have to bring your own car or booster seat, as the taxi service will not provide one for you. Also, tips are greatly appreciated, usually around fifteen percent of the fare.

If getting around Anguilla by taxi is not your first option for transportation, there are plenty of other options out there. Most people, especially families vacationing on the island, end up renting a car during their stay. This is without question the most efficient method if you feel confident navigating unfamiliar roads on your own.Catching a bus is unfortunately not an option, though large parties certainly have the opportunity to hire a small bus to drive them around. If you are traveling solo or with another adult, you may want to take the time to consider getting around by bike or moped. Learn how to do so by our Bike and Mopeds page in this book.

Traveling by taxi is a popular way to traverse this tropical island. Hailing a cab is just as easy as finding one, so leave the driving to someone else as you enjoy the beauty and adventure of Anguilla.

Travel Basics

Travel Fundamentals for Anguilla
Vacationers have much to learn before traveling to a foreign country
Although Anguilla is a small island, there is a large amount of information that travelers should know before they journey to this island paradise of pristine beaches and fine cuisine. Whether it is knowing how to call home or learning the location of the local embassy, travelers should brush up on the basics.

The intricacies of daily life in a foreign country can be different from what travelers experience at home. Vacationers never know what needs or occasions might arise during their trip to Anguilla, so they should gather as much information as they can about staying on the island. In addition to basic pieces of information such as custom laws and tourist offices, travelers should learn about the local etiquette and understand the various regions of the country.

Etiquette

Anguilla's charm comes from its stunning beaches and the island's many friendly residents. Exchanging greetings and other pleasantries is an important part of daily life on the island, and vacationers should never fail to reciprocate with an acknowledgment, response, and smile.

Dress is another important custom and matter of etiquette in the Caribbean. While travelers may lounge in their beachwear and skimpy clothing on the beach or at the pool, these types of clothing are considered highly inappropriate in other locations such as restaurants, shops, streets, and towns. Nice restaurants will expect their guests to be dressed sharply. There are no nude beaches in Anguilla, and going topless is not permitted.

Although Anguilla will produce many excellent photo opportunities, travelers should always ask permission before pointing their camera at a person or a their home, shop, or other possession. This general rule of etiquette applies throughout the Caribbean. Thousands of tourists bring their cameras to Anguilla every year, and it is a simple matter of courtesy and respect to ask permission. Occasionally, residents may expect a small monetary tip for the picture.

Finally, try to be respectful of the local culture and environment by treating the people and land with respect. Your displays of kindness and courtesy will ensure that you fit in perfectly in Anguilla.

Regions

At just 16 miles long and 3 miles wide, Anguilla is a small island with a limited number of regions. Getting from one spot to another by rental car or taxi should be easy.

Region	Description
The Valley	Located in the center of the island, this is the capital of Anguilla. The government is located here, as are the post office and banks. The Wallblake Airport, is located just to the south of The Valley.
To the Southwest	To the west of The Valley lie a number of the island's most popular beaches, as well as the famous and nearly deserted Sandy Island. Shoal Bay West, Rendezvous Bay, and Maunday's Bay all have alluring beaches. Ferry and cruise ship travelers call at Blowing Point Harbour.
To the Northeast	The northeast section of the island also has a number of beautiful beaches, as well as several dive sites and offshore islands. Shoal Bay, located west of Island Harbour, is a famous beach destination in the Caribbean. Offshore islands include Sicily Cay and Scrub Island.

The people and beaches of Anguilla, surrounded by the intoxicating blue waters of the Caribbean, will make travelers wish they never had to leave this small tropical island.

Clothing

Clothing and Attire in Anguilla

Dressing appropriately in Anguilla is a breeze, but don't forget to respect local customs

Choosing the right items to bring on your tropical vacation to Anguilla means packing clothing appropriate for the weather and culture.

Since the island maintains a tropical climate almost all year long, you'll probably want to bring light comfortable clothing along with plenty of beach wear for long days of sunbathing and swimming in the beautiful blue waters of the Caribbean.

During the warm and sunny days, travelers may want to wear light materials such as comfortable cottons. It is never actually cold in Anguilla, but the island breezes can get slightly cooler in the evenings. You may want to bring light sweater or jacket in case you get chilly. The island sometimes experiences short, unexpected showers, especially in the winter months. Storms generally come in short bursts, and sparkling sunshine soon follows. Pack umbrellas and rain gear that aren't too cumbersome, so you can quickly put them away after the rain.

Anguilla's beaches are one of the main reasons that tourists visit the island, so bringing adequate beach wear is definitely a must. Swimsuits and trunks are appropriate at the beach and around hotel swimming pools, but bikini tops and going shirtless is generally frowned upon in towns, shops, restaurants, and other common areas. Definitely pack a cover-up while walking around the grounds of your hotel or resort. The island has an overall casual atmosphere, so shorts for both men and women are acceptable for almost every event. If you're going to dine at a fancy restaurant, travelers should wear dressy casual attire, such as a nice slacks or a sun dress.

If you're invited to an island party or function, be sure to inquire about the social setting. If the event is casual, men should wear a pair of nice slacks, but no tie. If the event is formal, men should sport a tie and women should wear a nice dress. If the affair is black-tie, men should wear a jacket or blazer and women should dress up.

Packing your clothing should be one of the easiest things you do in preparation for your getaway to amazing Anguilla. Simply imagine yourself at each setting you hope to encounter, and you'll know exactly what to wear.

Currency

Anguilla's currency options
Knowing what kinds of payment are accepted can make your vacation a lot easier
When traveling to a foreign country, it's important to understand the currency exchange between your home country and your destination.

Anguilla's local currency is the Eastern Caribbean dollar, which is fixed to the U.S. dollar at $2.72(EC) to $1(USD). The U.S. dollar is accepted pretty much everywhere on the island.

While visiting Anguilla, you can receive change in either U.S. dollars or Eastern Caribbean dollars, or even both. Airports and hotels have currency exchanges, but go to a bank to get the best rates. Before leaving your home country, exchange some money for travel incidentals such as tipping at the airport and ground transportation to your accommodations. This is good advice for U.S. citizens, as well. Even though most places accept U.S. currency, it's always good to be prepared in case something out of the ordinary happens. You don't want to worry about getting Eastern Caribbean money while you're trying to get settled in.

The following chart details some of Anguilla's currency exchange rates with other countries as of February 10, 2005:

Country's Monetary Unit	U.S. $	E.C. $
British Pound	1.64	4.45
Canadian Dollar	1.06	2.88
European Union Euro	1.45	3.93
Japanese Yen	0.01	0.03
Swiss Franc	1.25	3.38

Most major businesses, hotels, and restaurants on Anguilla accept all major credit cards, but it's a good idea to call ahead and ask to be sure. You may run into trouble trying to pay with a personal check, so you should always have cash or a credit card to cover your bill.

Customs

Getting Through Customs in Anguilla
Abiding by customs and regulations can help you avoid travel delays

A vacation on the beautiful island of Anguilla should be a wonderful and unforgettable experience. Though you may want to head straight for the beach when you arrive, there a few processes that you must go through before gaining access to all of Anguilla's glory.

Going through island customs should not be a difficult ordeal for most travelers. By following a few basic guidelines, you can ensure a smooth arrival and departure from your vacation paradise.

For the most part, Anguilla's immigration and customs officers are friendly and helpful and can answer most travelers' questions. But keep in mind that these officers are there to enforce strict regulations and requirements on importing and exporting certain goods to and from the island. Anguilla's custom laws take effect as soon as you begin your travels to the island, so it is important to know what items can be brought into the country and what articles are prohibited. There are severe penalties for bringing contraband and restricted items to Anguilla, and persons who smuggle illegal drugs or other goods in excess of the island's allowance will face serious prosecution.

Visitors to the island can bring personal items into the country, including one quart of alcohol, one half pound of tobacco, foods, and already used clothing. Here are some other customs specifics to remember when traveling to Anguilla:

> When arriving on Anguilla by private boat, travelers must clear Customs and Immigration located at Blowing Point or at Road Bay.

> Pets are generally more comfortable in their home surroundings, and traveling may put them under a great deal of stress. But if you're going to bring your pet on vacation be sure to plan ahead. Six months prior to your planned vacation, contact the Agricultural Department at 264-497-2615 or the island veterinarian at 264-497-4600. Remember, only certain pets are allowed on Anguilla, and individual hotels may have their own restrictions.

> If you love the island of Anguilla so much that you decide to relocate there, you should contact the Immigration Department at 264-497-2451.

Travelers returning from Anguilla will also have to clear customs of their home country. United States citizens may bring original artwork, antiques, up to 200 cigarettes, and up to 100 non-Cuban cigars duty-free. Additional U.S. customs regulations follow:

➢ Travelers at least 21 years of age can bring back up to two liters of alcohol duty-free, as long as one liter of it was made in a CBI (Caribbean Basin Initiative) country.

➢ If you have stayed on Anguilla for at least 48 hours, you can bring back up to $600(USD) in goods, as long as you haven't used this exemption in the past 30 days.

➢ You can mail gifts back home, but must limit this to one package per addressee per day.

➢ The contents of your package cannot contain tobacco, alcohol, or perfume worth more than $500(USD).

➢ Mark mailed goods worth $100(USD) as "Unsolicited Gift" and "Consolidated Gift Package".

Because custom laws are subject to change, travelers are advised to contact their customs agencies to stay up-to-date on the current customs regulations.

Country	Contact
United States	U.S. Customs Service Tel: 877-227-5511
United Kingdom	HM Customs and Excise Tel: 0-845-010-9000

	www.hmce.gov.uk
Australia	Australian Customs Service Tel: 1300-363-263 +61 (2) 6275 6666 www.customs.gov.au
Canada	Canada Customs and Revenue Agency Tel: 800-461-9999 204-983-3500 www.ccra-adrc.gc.ca
China	Customs General Administration Fax: 852-2542-3334 www.customs.gov.cn
New Zealand	New Zealand Customs Service Toll Free: 0 (800) 4 CUSTOMS (428-786) Fax: 9-359-6730 www.customs.govt.nz
Sweden	Swedish Customs Tel: +46 (0) 771 23 23 23 www.tullverket.se

Following customs guidelines will make your arrival and departure a simple process so you can enjoy the time of your life on Anguilla.

Driving

Roadway Guidance in Anguilla

Getting behind the wheel means taking a few necessary precautions

Driving is a great way to see the wonderful sites of Anguilla at your own speed. Vacationers who opt to drive on the island can get up and go whenever they choose.

While driving in Anguilla, tourists should keep a few things in mind to make their trip safe. While operating a vehicle in Anguilla, remember that driving is done on the left-hand side of the road, as in England. This can be a challenge for some, and these people often find that requesting a vehicle with the steering wheel on the right side of the vehicle is helpful in reminding them of their place on the street. This is important to do because many rental cars have the steering wheel on the left like most vehicles in the United States.

Though knowing which side of the road to drive on may take some getting used to, the overall experience of driving on Anguilla is a good one. This is thanks to the relatively flat topography. There are a few main roads that bisect one another, but there have been some complaints that they are not very well maintained. While this may be true of the main road that runs through the center of the island, there are a few newer roads on the north side of the island that are much smoother. If you aren't driving on a paved road, it'll be sand or dirt paths that you're navigating.

Also be aware that there are five roundabouts on the island in order to promote safe driving. They are called the "Sandy Ground Roundabout," the "Airport Roundabout," "The Valley Roundabout," the "Shoal Bay Roundabout," and the "Sandy Hill Roundabout." You enter them from the left, but don't let them make you nervous. It is rare to see more than one vehicle in a roundabout at a time.

Requirements

Before you set out to drive, you must have a valid driver's license from your home country and a local driving permit. Vacationers can get an Anguilla driving permit at the same **rental car** agency that they rent their vehicle from. Also note that most rental agencies require that you be over the age of 25 to rent from them.

Rules of the Road

Along with the basic requirements for driving on the island, travelers should remember a few simple tips to stay safe on the road. On most roadways, the speed limit is 30 mph, except in school zones and in villages where you'll have to slow down to at least 20 mph. Drivers should strictly observe the speed limit for the safety of themselves and those around them. Speed limit indications are usually easy-to-read circular signs outlined in red. If you become confused while driving, pull over and ask for assistance. A friendly local will surely be able to help you and point you in the right direction.

Safety Tips

While you're keeping an eye out for pedestrians, you may also want to be alert for kids crossing the road - and not just the human ones. Anguilla is full of free-roaming goats, who often wander into the middle of the road. Children are also known for doing the same thing. There are no sidewalks on the island, so pedestrians have to walk on the edge the road. Be especially careful at night time, as it may hard to see someone - or something - walking along the road.

Pay attention to speed bumps. Going over one too quickly can cause a painful little jolt and may even damage your vehicle. Speed bumps are particularly prevalent near villages, so look for warning signs and slow down when approaching these "sleeping policemen," who are meant to control traffic speed.

Vehicle related injuries are the leading cause of children traveling abroad. Make sure that if you are traveling with a small child you bring with you the proper safety restraint system required, be it a booster or car seat.

More Transportation Options

If you're not up for driving on your own, there are other options for getting around available to you in Anguilla. The public transportation system is not very extensive, so if you imagine yourself traveling from place to place by bus, you'll have to actually hire one yourself. This is only a sound idea for large parties. Smaller groups will do better ordering a taxi service, and you can even hire your driver for a two hour tour for around $40(USD) a person, plus $5(USD) for each additional passenger.

Driving can be an excellent way to experience Anguilla, but don't forget to put safety first and to fill up your tank at any of the island's gas stations while you're out exploring this magnificent Caribbean island.

Electricity

Outlets and Voltage in Anguilla
Anguilla's electrical current may come as a pleasantly shocking surprise to some

Many travelers visiting the little island of Anguilla will find that plugging in their electrical appliances is less of a hassle than on many other Caribbean islands.

Almost all of Anguilla uses North American-style 110-volt power current, which is very convenient for travelers from the United States and Canada.

Power on the island is provided solely by the Anguilla Electricity Company Limited, which supplies reliable electricity at 120 volts AC on 60 cycles. If you're bringing appliances made in either the U.S. or Canada, you'll more than likely be able to plug them in with no problems. Electricity, as well as the electrical outlets, are the same as in both Canada and the United States. If you're visiting Anguilla from another country, you will probably have to purchase an adapter or transformer. Some hotels have transformers available when you arrive, but it is always a good idea to find out ahead of time.

The wattage on Anguilla may or may not be the same as in your home country, but planning ahead and purchasing the right electrical conversion equipment will ensure that you have virtually no problems plugging in your appliances.

Embassies

Embassies and Consulates in Anguilla
Embassies and consulates provide aid to travelers in need
Although it is unlikely that travelers will encounter civil unrest or crime during their stay in Anguilla, natural disasters and medical emergencies can be cause for concern. In times of need, travelers can turn to their local embassy or consular agent for help.

Located at the north of the Leeward Islands, Anguilla can be subject to Atlantic hurricanes and tropical storms. These powerful storms can cause significant damage to the island's facilities and can result in the loss of life. In the aftermath of these natural disasters, embassies and consulates can help locate travelers and give them medical and financial assistance.

Although embassies and consulates are not doctors or hospitals, officials can direct travelers to appropriate medical services. Travelers should always consider purchasing travel medical insurance that will cover an emergency evacuation flight.

Although crime is rare, consular agents can assist travelers in securing legal, financial, or medical assistance. If a traveler is accused of a crime, consular agents can help them to secure legal representation and will ensure that prison conditions and treatment are humane.

Most countries advise their travelers to consult travel notes and warnings before traveling to a particular country. Travelers from the United States can read the Bureau of Consular Affairs tips for safe travel "http://travel.state.gov/travel/tips/safety" and should also consider registering their trip with the State Department (https://travelregistration.state.gov/ibrs/ui/).

Embassies and Consulates Serving Anguilla

Embassy or Consulate	Contact Information
United States Embassy in Barbados	Canadian Imperial Bank of Commerce Building Broad Street, Bridgetown, Barbados 246-436-4950 (main hotline) 246-431-0225 (consular section) http://bridgetown.usembassy.gov E-mail: consularbridge2@state.gov United States citizens traveling to Anguilla can register

	their trip. Visit: http://bridgetown.usembassy.gov https://travelregistration.state.gov/ibrs/ui/
United States Consulate in Antigua	Bluff House, Pigeon Point, English Harbour Juliet Ryder 268-463-6531 E-mail: ryderj@candw.ag
United Kingdom	Government House Anguilla 264-497-2621 (Governor) 264-497-2621 (Staff Officer) 264-497-3314 (Fax) E-mail: governorsoffice@gov.ai
Canadian High Commission in Barbados	The Canadian High Commission Bishop's Court Hill Bridgetown, Barbados 246-429-3550 246-429-3780 (Fax) http://www.dfait-maeci.gc.ca/barbados/menu-en.asp E-mail: bdgtn@international.gc.ca
Australian High Commission on Trinidad and Tobago	18 Herbert Street St Clair Port of Spain 868-628-4732 868-622-0659 (Fax)

Embassies of the United Kingdom throughout the world

Embassy or Consulate	Contact Information
British Embassy - Washington, DC	3100 Massachusetts Avenue, NW Washington, DC 20008 202-588-6500 (Embassy) 202-588-7800 (Consular) 202-588-7830 (British council) 202-588-7850 (Consular Fax) http://www.britainusa.com/
British Consulate General - Atlanta, GA	Georgia Pacific Center Suite 3400 133 Peachtree Street, NE Atlanta, GA 30303 404-954-7700 404-954-7702 (Fax) http://www.britainusa.com/atlanta/
British Consulate General - Boston, MA	One Memorial Drive, 15th Floor Cambridge, MA 02142 617-245-4500 617-621-0220 (Fax) http://www.britainusa.com/boston/ E-mail: british.consulate@boston.mail.fco.gov.uk
British Honorary Consul - Charlotte, NC	330 South Tryon Street Suite 400 Charlotte, NC 28202 704-383-4359 704-383-6545 (Fax) http://www.britainusa.com/consular/nc/ E-mail: mdteden@bellsouth.net

British Consulate General - Chicago, IL	The Wrigley Building 400 N. Michigan Avenue Suite 1380 Chicago, IL 60611 312-970-3800 312-970-3852 (Fax) 312-970-3854 (Consular/Visa Fax) http://www.britainusa.com/chicago/
British Consulate General - Denver, CO	Suite 1030, World Trade Centre Tower 1675 Broadway Denver, CO 80202 303-592-5200 303-592-5209 (Fax) http://www.britainusa.com/denver/ E-mail: John.Maguire@britcondenver.com
British Consulate General - Houston, TX	Wells Fargo Plaza 1000 Louisiana Suite 1900 Houston, TX 77002 713-659-6270 713-659-7094 (Fax) http://www.britainusa.com/houston/ E-mail: bcg.houston@fco.gov.uk
British Consulate General - Los Angeles, CA	11766 Wilshire Boulevard, Suite 1200 Los Angeles, CA 90025-6538 310-481-0031 310-481-2900 (Visa) 310-481-2960 (Fax) 310-481-2961 (Visa Fax) http://www.britainusa.com/la/

	E-mail: visas.losangeles@fco.gov.uk
British Consulate General - Miami, FL	Suite 2800 Brickell Bay Office Tower 1001 Brickell Bay Drive Miami, FL 33131 305-374-1522 305-374-8196 http://www.britainusa.com/miami/
British Consulate General - New York, NY	845 Third Avenue New York, NY 10022 212-745-0200 212-745-0200 (consular) 212-754-3062 (Fax) http://www.britainusa.com/ny/
British Consulate General - Orlando, FL	Suite 2110 Sun Trust Center 200 South Orange Avenue Orlando, FL 32801 407-581-1540 407-581-1550 (Fax) http://www.britainusa.com/orlando/
British Honorary Consulate - Philadelphia, PA	33rd Floor 1818 Market Street Philadelphia, PA 19103 215-557-7665 215-557-6608
British Consulate - Puerto Rico	Torre Chardon, Suite 1236 350 Chardon Avenue San Juan, Puerto Rico 00918

	787-758-9828
	787-758-9809 (Fax)
	E-mail: btopr1@coqui.net
British Consulate General - San Francisco, CA	Suite 850, 1 Sansome Street San Francisco, CA 94104 415-617-1300 415-434-2018 (Fax) http://www.britainusa.com/sf/
British Consulate - Seattle, WA	900 Fourth Ave, Suite 3100 Seattle, WA 98164 206-622-9255 206-622-4728 (Fax) http://www.britainusa.com/seattle/
British High Commission in Canada	80 Elgin Street Ottawa K1P 5K7 613-237-1530 613-237-7980 (Fax) 613-232-2533 (Visa Fax) 613-237-6537 (Passport Fax) E-mail: generalenquiries@BritaininCanada.org
British Consulate General - Montreal	Suite 4200 1000 De La Gauchetiere West Montreal Quebec H3B 4W5 514-866-5863 514-866-0202 (Fax) E-mail: bcgmtl@bellnet.ca
British Honorary Consul	Suite 700 1150 Claire Fontaine

- Quebec City	Quebec City Quebec G1R 5G4 418-521-3000 418-521-3099 (Fax)
British Consulate General - Toronto	777 Bay Street Suite 2800 College Park Toronto Ontario M5G 2G2 416-593-1290 416-593-1229 (Fax) http://www.uktradeinvestcanada.org/ E-mail: Britcon.Toronto@fco.gov.uk
British High Commission in Australia	Commonwealth Avenue Yarralumla Canberra 61-2-6270-6666 61-2-6273-3236 (Fax) E-mail: bhc.canberra@mail.uk.emb.gov.au
British High Commission in New Zealand	44 Hill Street Wellington 1 Mailing Address: P O Box 1812 Wellington 64-4-924-2888 64-4-924-2810 (Fax) http://www.britain.org.nz E-mail: PPA.Mailbox@fco.gov.uk

	E-mail: bhc.wel@xtra.co.nz
	visamail.wellington@fco.gov.uk
	passportmail.wellington@fco.gov.uk
	consularmail.wellington@fco.gov.uk
British Embassy in Paris	35 rue du Faubourg St Honoré
	75383 Paris Cedex 08
	33-1-44-51-31-00
	33-1-44-51-31-27 (Consular Fax)
	http://ukinfrance.fco.gov.uk/en/
	E-mail: webmaster@amb-grandebretagne.fr
British Embassy in the Netherlands	Lange Voorhout 10
	2514 ED The Hague
	31-(0)-70-4270-427
	31-70-427-0345 (Fax)
	http://www.britain.nl
	E-mail: library@fco.gov.uk
British High Commission in Antigua	PO Box 483
	Price Waterhouse Centre
	11 Old Parham Rd
	St John's
	268-462-0008
	268-562-2124 (Fax)
	E-mail: britishc@candw.ag

Although there are no consulates or embassies stationed on the small island of Anguilla, travelers can contact local representatives of their government on neighboring islands. Travelers in need should take advantage of these important contacts when traveling to Anguilla or abroad.

Health

Staying Healthy in Anguilla

Medical facilities on the island are limited, but health risks are few and often preventable

Visiting a foreign country exposes travelers to new environments and potential new health concerns. Travelers should keep in mind a few medical tips to stay healthy while vacationing on the alluring island of Anguilla.

If you are traveling to Anguilla with prescription medication, make sure to keep the medication in their original, clearly marked container, packed alongside a prescription slip and note from your physician detailing the condition which causes you to depend upon the medication. This will make it clear the customs officials that you need the medicine, and prevent them from confiscating the drugs.

One of the main safety concerns while vacationing on Anguilla is overexposure to the elements. Spending time on the island's beautiful beaches can make for a wonderful time, but can also cause serious health problems if you're not careful. Here are a few tips to make having fun in the sun safe:

- ➤ Always remember to wear adequate sunscreen to protect your skin from the scorching sun's harmful rays. Also consider wearing sunglasses, hats, and protective coverings to beat back the sun.

- ➤ To avoid overheating, dehydration, and sun stroke, remember to drink plenty of liquids, especially water.

Probably one of the most unexpected dangers on the island lies in the form of a tree. The poisonous manchineel tree is sometimes found on Anguilla's beaches, and tourist should avoid touching this hazardous plant. Mosquitoes and other bugs can be a pesky nuisance and a danger to your health. Avoid nasty bug bites by using bug spray and wearing long clothing when spending time outdoors.

Travelers aren't required to receive specific vaccinations prior to visiting the island, but they should be up to date on their routine immunizations, as well Hepatitis A and B.

Travelers should check with their insurance providers to find out if they'll be covered overseas. Anguilla has only one major hospital, so any major medical issues will probably require evacuation, which may or may not be covered under your policy. Medical evacuation can cost tens of thousands of dollars, so its always a good idea to find out what your insurance company covers. Consider purchasing travel insurance to supplement your coverage. Also, don't forget to bring a copy of your insurance ID card, claims forms, and other relevant insurance documents.

If you need emergency medical attention, you can go to Anguilla's Princess Alexandra College, which is located in Sandy Ground. Anguilla also has clinics in major settlements, and ambulance and emergency room service around the clock. For emergencies, dial "911" from anywhere on the island.

For any other small incidents, it is wise to have a Travel Medical Kit at your disposal. This should include the following items:

- ➢ Painkillers including acetaminophen, aspirin, ibuprofen;
- ➢ Antihistamines;
- ➢ Topical disinfectant;
- ➢ Antacids;
- ➢ Rubbing alcohol;
- ➢ Bandages;
- ➢ Thermometer.

Though a medical emergency is not likely to occur during your Anguilla vacation, it is always best to arrive knowledgeable of any possible health concerns and prepared to handle anything.

Hours of Operation

Have the Time of Your Life in Anguilla

Shops and businesses in Anguilla may have different business hours during certain times of year

During the high tourist season, travelers will find that Anguilla's business hours are mostly convenient on the weekdays, while most places close early on the weekends. For the low tourist season, however, it's a completely different story.

Because there are very few tourists visiting the island during the summer months, many local businesses close earlier, and some even shut down completely. Vacationers can avoid missing out on great shopping or taking care of business by knowing what time banks, government offices, and other facilities close.

Banks

Travelers can take care of monetary matters at any of the banks located around the island. For the most part, all banks follow the same business hours and are open Monday through Thursday from 8:00 a.m. to 3:00 p.m., and on Friday from 8:00 a.m. to 5:00 p.m. Generally, all banks are closed on the weekends and during the island's major holidays.

Shops

Anguilla isn't particularly known for its outstanding shopping outlets. Many of the island's shops are scattered among local villages and are not within easy walking distance of each other. But travelers who don't mind doing a little digging can locate some of the island's great souvenirs. Commercial businesses are generally open Monday through Friday from 8:00 a.m. to 5:00 p.m., and on Saturday from 8:00 a.m. to Noon.

Anguilla's business hours are all subject to change, especially between the high and low seasons. If you're unsure when a particular establishment is open, you can always call ahead.

Languages

Can We Talk in Anguilla?
Language is an important concern when traveling to a foreign country
On occasion, the most complicated part of taking a vacation can be communicating with local residents. Language barriers can make even small business transactions difficult for travelers. Luckily, many travelers will have no problem communicating in Anguilla.

Travelers from the United Kingdom, North America, Australia, and many other parts of the world should have no problem speaking the official language of Anguilla: English. While many of the islands in the Caribbean have strong Dutch or French roots, Anguilla is a part of the British West Indies and retains the language of those who settled there over 400 years ago. Although English is the official language of

Anguilla, travelers are likely to encounter a significant West Indian accent within the language

While travelers who only speak English may have difficulties with the Dutch, French, and Spanish spoken on other Caribbean islands, they should feel comfortable in Anguilla. Vacationers may wish to take advantage of the shared language by seizing the opportunity to speak with the island's friendly residents. Learn about local history or merely chat about island life with your tour guide. The exchanging of pleasantries is important in Anguilla, and English speakers should be sure to engage in this custom.

Whether you are a fluent English speaker, or speak just enough of the language to get by, you should find the English-speaking residents of Anguilla to be friendly and welcoming.

Passports

What Do I Need to enter Anguilla?
Having the right paperwork will make for a smoother trip to and from Anguilla
With its fantastic weather, gorgeous beaches, and tranquil environment, it's not hard to see why Anguilla has been blooming as a popular tourist destination over the past few years.

Upon arriving in this intriguing paradise, travelers must present certain identification and documentation before being allowed to enter

Anguilla. Knowing what items to bring on your vacation will allow you to arrive and depart the island with very few delays.

Passports

All visitors arriving on the island of Anguilla must present a passport that is valid for at least six more months. U.S. citizens must ave a valid passport to travel to Caribbean Islands, including Anguilla. U.S. citizens will be required to present their passport upon return to the States. All travelers must also show proof of a return or onward ticket in order to gain access to Anguilla.

Visas

Citizens of the United States, the United Kingdom, and Canada do not need a visa to enter Anguilla, as long as they plan to stay in the country for no more than six months. Citizens of the following countries are required to present a visa before entering Anguilla:

Afghanistan	Georgia	Oman
Albania	Ghana	Pakistan
Algeria	Guinea	Papua New Guinea
Angola	Guinea-Bissau	Peru
Armenia	Guyana	Philippines
Azerbaijan	Haiti	Qatar
Bangladesh	India	Romania

Belarus	Indonesia	Russia
Benin	Iran	Rwanda
Bhutan	Iraq	Sao Tome & Principe
Bosnia-Herzegovina	Ivory Coast	Saudi Arabia
Bulgaria	Jamaica	Senegal
Burkina Faso	Jordan	Sierra Leone
Burundi	Kazakhstan	Somalia
Burma	Kenya	Sri Lanka
Cambodia	Kyrgyzstan	Sudan
Cameroon	Korea (North)	Suriname
Cape Verdi	Kuwait	Syria
Central African Republic	Laos	Taiwan
Chad	Lebanon	Tajikistan
China	Liberia	Tanzania
Columbia	Libya	Thailand
Comoros	Macedonia	Togo
Congo	Madagascar	Tunisia
Croatia	Maldives	Turkey
Cuba	Mali	Turkish Republic of Northern Cyprus
Djibouti	Mauritania	Turkmenistan
Dominican Republic	Mauritius	Uganda

Ecuador	Moldova	Ukraine
Egypt	Mongolia	United Arab Emirates
Equatorial Guinea	Morocco	Uzbekistan
Eritrea	Mozambique	Vietnam
Ethiopia	Myanmar	Yemen
Fiji	Nepal	Yugoslavia
Gabon	Niger	Zaire
The Gambia	Nigeria	

Those who are traveling to Anguilla for diplomatic or official business are exempt from visa requirements. You can contact the Anguilla tourist board to find out the rates for acquiring a visa.

Knowing Anguilla's customs policies and entry requirements will allow you to have a virtually hassle-free arrival and departure so you can focus on having fun.

Postal Services

Anguilla Post Card Madness

Stamp collectors are likely to be familiar with the postal service of Anguilla

While in Anguilla, you may wish to write a letter to a loved one or send important business documents with high priority. Anguilla has a post office and several international courier services through which to send mail and packages.

Anguilla's post office is located in its capital, The Valley, which is situated in the center of the island. The Valley is not far from any location on the island, but some hotels provide mail drop-off spots. Post office hours are Monday through Friday, 8:00 a.m. to 3:30 p.m.

Airmail to the United States and Canada generally takes about one or two weeks to reach its destination. Airmail to destinations in the United Kingdom and Europe may take three weeks. Letter and postcards to North America and Europe will cost around EC$1.50. Stamp booklets of varying combination can be bought from the post office for as little as EC$5.00.

The island also has several international courier services for sending packages and express mail, including FedEx, UPS, and DHL. FedEx is open Monday through Friday, 8:00 a.m. until 5:00 p.m., and Saturday, from 9:00 a.m. until 1:00 p.m. DHL is open from 8:00 a.m. until 5:00 p.m, Monday through Friday.

Organization	Contact Information
Post Office and Anguilla Philatelic Bureau	General Post Office The Valley Anguilla, British West Indies 264-497-2528

	Fax: 264-497-5455
	E-mail: angstamp@gov.ai
	http://www.aps.ai/
FedEx	Professional Courier Services (Anguilla) Ltd.
	The Hallmark Building
	Suite 227
	Old Airport Road, The Valley
	Anguilla, British West Indies
	264-497-3575
UPS	Keg's Sales & Agencies
	P.O. Box 1267
	George Hill
	West Indies
	Anguilla
	264-497-2680
	Fax: 264-497-2680
DHL	Sales Society Limited
	P.O Box 124
	Stoney Ground
	Anguilla, British West Indies
	264-497-3440

Stamps from Anguilla are popular with stamp collectors, and the Anguilla Philatelic Bureau frequently releases new issues. Popular collectible stamps have included the goats and hotels of Anguilla and stamps celebrating Prince William's 18th birthday.

Travelers should have no trouble staying in contact with loved ones and business associates as they relax in Anguilla due to the number of postal options available to them.

Telephones

Wanna Talk in Anguilla?
Calling home is a breeze from the island of Anguilla
Tourists should have no problem communicating by phone while in Anguilla. The island has a number of communication services available, including card phones, pay phones, and credit card calling facilities. All you have to do is pick up the phone and remember to dial a few simple numbers to get connected.

You can make a local call from almost anywhere on the island, including your hotel room and a pay phone. Hotels may charge a small fee for local calls, so you may want to inquire about this cost. You will also be charged for using the island's pay phones, and many tourists find that purchasing a calling card cuts down on the costs of both local and international calls.

Phone cards can be purchased at many locations on the island, including drug stores, the airport, and Cable & Wireless, which is open on the weekdays from 8:00 a.m. to 6:00 p.m., on Saturday from 9:00 a.m. to 1:00 p.m., and on Sunday from 10:00 a.m. to 2:00 p.m. These Caribbean phone cards can be used in specially marked phone booths.

You can also rent cellular phones for about $10(USD) per day at the Cable & Wireless local office, or purchase a pre-paid cell phone to use while in Anguilla at Digicel Anguilla. You can locate a Digicel retailer by contacting their customer care number at 264-498-DIGI.

Vacationers can make international phone calls from most phones, including hotel phones and pay phones. Hotels often have very expensive international rates for making direct overseas calls from your room. To place a local call, dial the seven-digit number. To call Anguilla from the United States, dial "1" plus the area code "264", plus the local seven-digit number. When calling Anguilla from the United Kingdom, dial "001", the area code, and the local seven-digit number. To call the island from Australia and New Zealand, dial "0011", then "1", then the area code and the number.

To call the U.S. or Canada from Anguilla, dial "1", the area code, and the seven-digit. To reach the U.K., dial "011", "44", and the local number. To call Australia, dial "011", "61", and the local number. And to reach New Zealand, dial "011", "64", and the local number.

Just because you are vacationing in another country does not mean you have to disconnect from your friends and family back home. Whether you purchase a phone card or pay long-distance rates from your hotel room, your loved ones are only a phone call away.

Time Zones

Got the Time in Anguilla?

Travelers may find that they lose their sense of time in beautiful Anguilla

Foreign travelers should plan on quickly forgetting their jet lag upon arrival in Anguilla. A watch is the last thing that vacationers will be looking at as the brilliant Caribbean sun reflects off the white sand and blue waters of Anguilla's 33 breathtaking beaches.

Like much of the Caribbean, this overseas territory of the United Kingdom is on Atlantic Standard Time. This time zone places Anguilla four hours behind Greenwich Mean Time, and four or five hours behind London and the rest of the United Kingdom. Travelers visiting Anguilla from most of mainland Europe will experience a time change of five to six hours, depending on the time of the year.

Unlike the United States and other locations, Anguilla does not observe daylight savings time. When daylight savings time is not being observed from October to April, Atlantic Standard Time is one hour ahead of the Eastern Standard Time observed on the east coast of the United States, and four hours ahead of the Pacific Standard Time observed on the West Coast. During daylight savings time, from April to October, Atlantic Standard Time matches Eastern Standard Time and is three hours ahead of Pacific Standard Time. Travelers from North America will experience very little time change as they travel to Anguilla. Daylight savings period was extended from March to

November, meaning that the east coast of the United States will be on the same time as Anguilla throughout most of the year.

World Wide Time Comparison for Anguilla

At Noon In Anguilla	
City	Local Time
Amsterdam	5:00 p.m. (plus 1 hour in daylight savings)
Brussels	5:00 p.m. (plus 1 hour in daylight savings)
Hong Kong	Midnight (next day)
Istanbul	6:00 p.m. (plus 1 hour in daylight savings)
Los Angeles	8:00 a.m. (plus 1 hour in daylight savings)
London	4:00 p.m. (plus 1 hour in daylight savings)
Madrid	5:00 p.m. (plus 1 hour in daylight savings)
Moscow	7:00 p.m. (plus 1 hour in daylight savings)
Paris	5:00 p.m. (plus 1 hour in daylight savings)
Sydney	3:00 a.m. (minus 1 hour in daylight savings)

Although time is likely to fly by in such a beautiful island setting, travelers should cherish every moment on Anguilla.

Tipping

Got the Time in Anguilla?

Travelers may find that they lose their sense of time in beautiful Anguilla

Foreign travelers should plan on quickly forgetting their jet lag upon arrival in Anguilla. A watch is the last thing that vacationers will be looking at as the brilliant Caribbean sun reflects off the white sand and blue waters of Anguilla's 33 breathtaking beaches.

Like much of the Caribbean, this overseas territory of the United Kingdom is on Atlantic Standard Time. This time zone places Anguilla four hours behind Greenwich Mean Time, and four or five hours behind London and the rest of the United Kingdom. Travelers visiting Anguilla from most of mainland Europe will experience a time change of five to six hours, depending on the time of the year.

Unlike the United States and other locations, Anguilla does not observe daylight savings time. When daylight savings time is not being observed from October to April, Atlantic Standard Time is one hour ahead of the Eastern Standard Time observed on the east coast of the United States, and four hours ahead of the Pacific Standard Time observed on the West Coast. During daylight savings time, from April to October, Atlantic Standard Time matches Eastern Standard Time and is three hours ahead of Pacific Standard Time. Travelers from North America will experience very little time change as they travel to Anguilla. Daylight savings period was extended from March to November, meaning that the east coast of the United States will be on the same time as Anguilla throughout most of the year.

World Wide Time Comparison for Anguilla

At Noon In Anguilla	
City	Local Time
Amsterdam	5:00 p.m. (plus 1 hour in daylight savings)
Brussels	5:00 p.m. (plus 1 hour in daylight savings)
Hong Kong	Midnight (next day)
Istanbul	6:00 p.m. (plus 1 hour in daylight savings)
Los Angeles	8:00 a.m. (plus 1 hour in daylight savings)
London	4:00 p.m. (plus 1 hour in daylight savings)
Madrid	5:00 p.m. (plus 1 hour in daylight savings)
Moscow	7:00 p.m. (plus 1 hour in daylight savings)
Paris	5:00 p.m. (plus 1 hour in daylight savings)
Sydney	3:00 a.m. (minus 1 hour in daylight savings)

Although time is likely to fly by in such a beautiful island setting, travelers should cherish every moment on Anguilla.

Tourist Offices

It's Good to Know
Finding information about Anguilla is no problem with the help of so many tourist offices

Vacationers can get information about Anguilla before they depart and once they arrive on the island.

Many travelers will have questions about their vacation on this beautiful Caribbean island. Tourist offices are great places to find expert information and advice.

Tourists can get travel brochures and other kinds of information from Anguilla tourist offices, which have many locations around the world. Here are some offices located in several different countries:

Tourist Office	Contact Information
The Anguilla Tourist Board	Coronation Avenue The Valley, Anguilla, BWI 1-800-553-4939 264-497-2759 264-497-2710 (Fax) Email: atbtour@anguillanet.com
United States	Anguilla Tourist Board Marketing Office 111 Decatur Street Doylestown, PA 18901 Tel.: 267-880-3511 Fax: 267-880-3507 Email: enterprisefx@aol.com anguillabwi@aol.com
United Kingdom	Carolyn Brown Anguilla Tourist Board 7a Crealock Street London SW18 2BS 011-44-208-871-0012 011-44-207-207-4323 (Fax)

	Email: Anguilla@tiscali.co.uk
Canada	William & Sari Marshalls
	116C Hazelton Avenue
	Toronto, Canada M5R 2E4
	416-944-8105
	416-944-3191 (Fax)
	Email: xybermedia@aol.com
France	Gerard Germin
	Anguilla Tourist Board
	c/o Sergat Sarl
	745 av. Du General Leclerc
	92100 Boulgne Billancourt, France
	011-33-1-4608-5984
	011-33-1-4609-9676 (Fax)
	Email: anguillaparis@wanadoo.fr
Germany	Anguilla Tourist Board
	c/o Sergat Deutschland
	IM Guldenen Wingert 8-C
	D-64342 Seeheim, Germany
	011-49-6257-962920
	011-49-6257-962919 (Fax)
	Email: r.morozow@sergat.de
Italy	Stefano DePaoli
	DePaoli Associati Communications
	Via del Marc 4720142
	Milano, Italy
	011-39-0289-534108
	011-39-0284-60841 (Fax)
	Email: anguilla@depaoliassociati.com

Monaco/Spain	Antionio Orzcovilla
	c/o Jet Travel
	Le Coronado
	20 Av.de Fontvieille
	MC 98000 Monaco
	011-377-97-98-41-22
	011-377-97-98-41-20 (Fax)
	Email: antionio@jet-travel.com
Puerto Rico	Guillermo Pino
	Box 11850, Suite #451
	San Juan, PR 00922-1850
	787-647-4420
	787-783-9388 (Fax)
	Email: atbpuertorico@yahoo.com

Planning an exciting trip to Anguilla can be made a little bit easier with the help of these international tourist offices.

Weather

Learn About the Weather of Anguilla

Anguilla's weather is consistently arid and tropical throughout the year

The weather in Anguilla is perfect almost all year long, which makes the island a popular vacation destination for thousands of sun-loving travelers. Tourists should expect great weather while visiting this gorgeous island, but should also be prepared for unexpected forecasts, like rainstorms.

The warm tropical temperatures on the island are moderated by breezes from the northeast tradewinds. These refreshing currents make a hot day at the beach a little more comfortable, so you won't be overwhelmed by the sun's sultry rays. Always remember to drink plenty of fluids and wear adequate amounts of sunscreen to protect your skin from harmful UV rays.

Anguilla's year-round temperatures hardly ever get below a lovely 70 degrees Fahrenheit, even in the winter time. Travelers can expect highs lingering in the mid 80s on toasty summer days. Because of its location near the equator, temperatures here don't vary drastically throughout the year. Therefore, Anguilla's seasons are based on the amount of rain, resulting in a dry and a rainy season.

Arid is the best way to describe the island of Anguilla, which lacks rainforests and mountainous regions. The little island is limited in its agricultural production, and the sparse soil produces a few fields of corn and peas. During the summer time, the island experiences low pressure systems that can bring a few showers and clouds. But for the most part, rainstorms are few in number and don't last for more than a few minutes. The island gets even less rain during the winter months. Average yearly rainfall is just 35 inches, which is great news for travelers who want to spend time lounging on the island's beautiful beaches.

Anguilla's terrain is mostly flat and featureless, with no high mountainous or hilly areas. Unlike many other islands in the Caribbean, it has no high altitudes and few rainforests, so temperatures are pretty much the same all over the island. During the summer, from the months of June to November, Anguilla is faced with the hurricane season. Although it is generally safe to stay on the island during this time of year, travelers should always keep an eye on weather reports and storms that may be developing in the ocean. Vacationers should bring adequate rain gear in case of an unexpected island shower or storm, which generally last just a few minutes before the sun is shining brightly again.

Planning a vacation to the island of Anguilla means preparing for even the smallest details, like the weather. Vacationers will find this tropical paradise to be a wonderful vacation spot because of its gorgeous coastline and outstanding weather, making it perfect for a day on the beach and other island excursions. When visiting Anguilla, travelers can expect ample sunshine and very little humidity. But don't forget to bring rain gear for a sudden shower, and be aware of weather reports so you can make the most of your tropical getaway.

Month	Avg. Daily Temp (Degrees Fahrenheit)
January	78.6
February	78.6
March	79.2
April	80.7
May	82.0
June	83.9
July	84.0
August	84.2
September	84.0
October	83.4
November	81.7
December	79.7
Annual	81.7

The End

CPSIA information can be obtained
at www.ICGtesting.com
Printed in the USA
BVHW051432060423
661870BV00014B/509

9 781715 758110